ALSO BY ROBERT FULGHUM

All I Really Need to Know I Learned in Kindergarten

It Was on Fire When I Lay Down on It

Maybe (Maybe Not)

Uh-Oh

From Beginning to End

TRUE

LOVE

Stories told to and by

ROBERT FULGHUM

HarperCollins*Publishers*

HarperCollins books may be purchased for educational, business,
or sales promotional use. For information please write: Special Markets
Department, HarperCollins Publishers, Inc., 10 East 53rd Street,
New York, NY 10022.

FIRST EDITION

Designed by Joel Avirom and Jason Snyder

Library of Congress Cataloging-in-Publication Data
True love: stories told to and by Robert Fulghum / Robert Fulghum,
collected with commentary by the author.—1st ed.

p. cm.

ISBN 0-06-018784-0

1. Love. 2. Love—Anecdotes. I. Fulghum, Robert.

BD436.T78 1997

306.7—dc21 96-44625

97 98 99 00 01 ❖/RRD 10 9 8 7 6 5 4 3 2 1

To Habitat for Humanity, founded on the principle that the ultimate grace is found in the simple admonition "Love one another." All the net royalties from the sale of this book are dedicated to its work.

Thanks

To all those who contributed to the making
of this book, with letters, stories, and advice.

To the hundreds of writers whose letters we did not print—
but whose thoughts helped shape the spirit of the book.

To Barbara Witt, Chief of Stuff of Fulghum Heavy Industries,
who did the hard work of managing the manuscript
from start to finish.

PERSPECTIVE

Tell me a love story.

Not one you've read or heard. One you've lived.

For several years I've been asking that of friends and strangers—first in my book Uh-Oh *and later in my newspaper column. The mail poured in from teenagers in the ecstatic pain of first love, from the elderly scrawling out sacred memories from retirement homes, from those who treasure a small forever based on a ten-second encounter, and from those whose love is measured in a lifetime of heartbeats. Mail came from thirty-six states and seven foreign countries. From writers age eight to age ninety-eight. From men and women, from straight and gay, from wise and foolish,* from confused and sane. Handwritten on expensive stationery, printed on yellow legal-pad paper, and impeccably turned out by computer. Hundreds and hundreds of letters.

I expected gooey-sweet greeting-card sentiments but got salty surprises—nasty love and crazy love as well. I expected bluebird-and-rainbow love, but also got stormy love with lightning and hail and landslides. I expected mushy oatmeal love but got just as much steak-and-potatoes love. I expected meek-and-mild love, but got as much love made out of muscle and bone and blood.

Intrigued by the mail, I went looking for love stories from those who don't like to write or don't have time. I made a sign: TELL ME A SHORT LOVE STORY AND I WILL BUY YOU COFFEE AND MAKE YOU FAMOUS and took the sign around to some of Seattle's neighborhood espresso houses, to a couple of bars, and to a neighborhood fair. The sign always drew a crowd—especially when people understood that the purpose of the love story project was to benefit Habitat for Humanity.

At first, getting people to talk candidly about love was a problem. More often than not, people would roll their eyes and laugh and say they had a love story, all right, but it wasn't short or sweet. With encouragement, they would tell the story anyhow, often entertaining our small audience with both the implausible plots of their stories and their skills as raconteurs.

Several people got standing ovations, drawing an even bigger crowd. "Hey, what's going on here?" "True love stories." "Really? I've got one you won't believe." And they did. Oddly enough, it is that quality of sheer unbelievability that makes a love story credible. If truth is stranger than fiction, then true love is even stranger.

Every story seemed to lead to another story. Closing a true-love storytelling session was much harder than getting one started. We've all been there. We'd all go back there, most likely.

On one occasion, a story was the beginning of a story yet to be told. A young woman listened enraptured as a young man told about being spurned in love. When he finished, she said she would never turn down a guy who felt that way about love. He wanted to know her story. They were still talking when I left. Who knows what happened next? In matters of love, everything is possible.

People sometimes said they had a story, but needed to get permission from someone else before they could share it. One example was a middle-aged man in suit and tie, carrying the Wall Street Journal *both times I met him. The second day he came back to give me a pale blue envelope—perfumed—the kind used for personal correspondence. He said, "Before you read this, you should know that I've had it for at least ten years, that it's from my wife, to whom I am still married." Inside the envelope was a matching sheet of stationery, with these words written with pen and ink:*

My dearest Harry:
I hate you, I hate you, I hate you.
Respectfully, with all my love, Edna.

I smiled and looked up, anticipating the rest of the story.

He smiled as he refolded the note and put it back in the envelope.

"That's it," he said, and walked away.

The shortest love story of all I collected is this one: From a waifish little girl of about four years, who stands by, staring at me, sucking her thumb and holding a raggedy yellow blanket up to her face.

"Do you love your blanket?"

Child nods her head—Yes.

"Does your blanket love you?"

Child shakes head impatiently—No, of course not.

The child is not confused about love. She knows already. It's mostly a thing between people. In fact, I was impressed by how wise most people are about love. These sentences, taken from letters and conversations, stand out:

"Love is what you've been through with someone."

"The reasons you fall into love are often the same reasons for falling out."

"There's a big difference between the first time you fall in love and the first time falling in love really matters."

"You can't get the exact love you want—only the love someone can give."

"Every love story is unique—love is not a group activity."

"Sex without love is a meaningless experience, but as meaningless experiences go, it's pretty high on the list."

I could go on—and will.

But first, read some of the stories.

Many of the stories begin in an ordinary way and end with a surprise. So surprising, in fact, that you may find yourself wondering if these stories really are true. I believe them. I know too much about real love not to. Everything anybody has ever said about love is true, just not all at once for all of us. Still, it's all true for somebody somewhere sometime. Love is the grand prize and the garbage heap. Love is a spiritual root canal and the only thing that makes life worth living. Love is a little taste of always and a big bite of nothing. And love is everything in between these extremes. It may be why there's that part in the wedding vows about "for better or worse; for richer, for poorer; in sickness and in health." It's the language of a realistic warranty for love.

The love we really live is all the love we really have.

And the love we really have is the love that's true.

CAVEAT

More than forty people reviewed this manuscript before publication. When I asked if they had any advice for the reader, the response was near unanimous. I pass it along to you:

Don't read this book straight on through.

Too much true love can cause heartburn.

These stories are best if read a few at a time.

And they're even better when read aloud to someone you love.

Here is the entire text of a love letter intercepted by a second-grade schoolteacher, passed on to a parent who passed it on to me:

> Dear Billy, if you dont say you love me and walk to the bus top with me I will kill myself and beet you up. I love you and wan to marry you soon. Susy.

The little girl was eight at the time. The parent showed me the letter when the girl was twenty-four. At a rehearsal dinner. The day before Susy married Billy. During the service, I shared the letter with the guests and, in her vows, had Susy repeat after me: "I, Susy, promise you, Billy, never to kill myself or beat you up."

If the marriage lasts as long as her love, and her love is as large as the laughter in the ceremony, the odds are good for happy ever after.

—a minister,
Bellevue, WA,
as told to R. F.

You wanted really short love stories. This one's long but small. I go to the Pike Place Market in Seattle almost every Saturday morning to shop and carry on a love affair.

For several years I've bought flowers from a youngish woman who is a refugee from one of the hill tribes of Indo-China. For one thing, she has the freshest and most beautiful flowers. For another, she is a fresh and beautiful flower herself. I don't know her name, nor she mine. We don't speak the same language. To her, I must be just another customer.

She is spring to me. She's there with pussy-willows, daffodils, and then irises. She's summer, with roses and sunflowers. She's fall, with dahlias and chrysanthemums. As the growing season comes to an end, she brings stems of fall leaves to sell, and then it's over. In winter, I miss her.

When we exchange flowers and money, I always try to briefly and slyly touch her hand. I always insist she keep the change and she always insists on giving me an extra flower.

Once I tried to buy all her flowers at once, but she just shook her head. "No." I don't know why. Maybe she, too, is in love with someone and wants to be there to sell him flowers when he comes.

—M. M., Seattle, WA

When I was a junior in college I took a course in the writing of D. H. Lawrence. I know this sounds really stupid, but I thought this was about Lawrence of Arabia, you know—the eccentric British desert warrior guy. I had seen the movie and I wanted to be him. I was not fully alert in college.

I went down to the local used book store to get everything they had. I was a little surprised by the titles: *The Rainbow, Women in Love, Sons and Lovers*, and *Lady Chatterley's Lover*. There was a side of Lawrence of Arabia I didn't know about. The clerk explained. Whoa. Bad news, but I had registered for the course and now I had the books and I needed the credits, so I was stuck. I went home to read.

Like a lot of college students, I bought used books hoping someone else would have already underlined the important stuff. The Lawrence books I bought were thoroughly underlined, and when I flipped through and read some of the paragraphs about making out, I was blown away. This was really hot stuff. To hell with the other Lawrence and the desert, this Lawrence was my kind of guy. And I figured that any girls who were taking this course would be my kind of girls.

All the books I bought had the same female name in the front. I figured this girl must have taken the course and then sold the books. She really knew what to underline—not only the juicy parts, but the really beautiful passages that were about love, not just sex. I looked her name up in the telephone book and she was there. I figured I'd just call her up and see what happened. I was hoping for anything from a date to copies of the papers she had written. College guys play all the angles.

I called her up, introduced myself and told her what I wanted. Whoa, again. She was not a girl but a retired college professor of English literature. These books were extras she had sold when she moved to a smaller apartment. She laughed and said she would be glad to have a date with me and she would explain about Lawrence and tell me how to pass the course.

We liked each other right away. She lived alone and her eyes were failing. She said if I would drive her to the grocery store once a week, she would tutor me in Lawrence. During that semester she woke me up about love and sexuality and women. I spent a lot of time with her. I'm a better man because of her. A long time later I told her if she had been 20 instead of 70 I would have asked her to marry me. She said she would have accepted. She's dead now. I still have her books and her wisdom and her kind of love. I got an A in the course, too.

—as told to R. F.

My dad paints my mom's toenails. I was there when he started doing it. The whole family was at a resort down in Oregon to celebrate my folks' fortieth wedding anniversary. My mom has always been a beauty queen ever since she won a pageant when she was in high school. She really is pretty and has very nice hands and feet, too. She likes makeup and facials and perfume and she always has had her fingernails and toenails painted. But when we were sitting out by the pool, I noticed for the first time that her toenails weren't done. I asked her why and she said she was getting too old and stiff to get down that far and she thought it was foolish to go to a beauty parlor to have it done.

My father is a big, gruff man's man who has coached football all his life. I was really surprised when he spoke up and told my mom he would be glad to paint her toenails for her. When she asked him why he would want to do a thing like that, he said, "It's because I love you and want you to feel beautiful as long as you live."

Five years later, he's still doing her toes for her.

—Myrna, Seattle, WA

It was the second summer my best friend and I went to the beach together. We had just turned fourteen and knew nothing of men, guys, boys, rats. We had been down at the beach for three days and her parents were going to let us go down to the boardwalk ALONE!!! They drove us down and we were ready for four hours of pure heaven. We had been walking around for about an hour when we spotted two guys we thought were perfect for us: they looked our age, they looked good, did they look at us?? Nah. Why would they look at us of all people? Another half hour passed, then so did they. Were they following us? Noooooo. This same thing kept on happening for about an hour or so: did they see us? Did they wave at us? Did we wave back?

Finally the guys had had enough. The next time we encountered each other they approached us. The one my friend and I decided I would "get" said, "Hi, I'm so-and-so and this is my friend so-and-so. We couldn't help but notice. . . ." I said, "I know, we couldn't help but notice either. My name is Katie and this is my friend Terry." "Hi," we all said in unison. OOOOOKKKKAAAAYYYYY.

Now what?? "Do you want to ride the roller-coaster?" so-and-so asked. "Sure," we did. So we bought tickets as two-somes. (So-and-so and I and Terry and so-and-so.) We rode the ride as two-somes, ate cotton candy as two-somes and broke apart into two-somes. Only this time our two-somes were unisex: Terry and I and our prospective summer loves. It was too bad actually. I still don't know how it happened. What became of this? Nothing, no address, no phone number, one summer later do I even remember their names? Nope.

What I do remember is how much fun I had that night and the following nights dreaming of what could or might happen.

MY PHILOSOPHY

This is how I think of love at age fifteen:

Love is 3/4 dream and 1/4 reality. Problems usually arise when you fall in love with the dream and not the reality. But, yet you find true love when you fall in love with both.

—Katie Ciccarello,
Ellicott City, MD

I was a sophomore in high school. She was a senior in college. I was impressing everyone with my expertise in German, since I had lived there four years while my father was in the service. She was impressing everyone with my ignorance, since she knew that I didn't really know what I thought I knew—and she was the student teacher.

It really made no difference to me. She was the most beautiful woman I had ever seen. Her wavy blonde hair rolled down over her shoulders the same way every time I saw her—it just seemed to stay that way. Her ocean deep blue eyes looked straight through me and transformed every moment she was near into pure tranquillity.

Since the town was small it was not unusual to run into her on occasion: at the grocery store, in the drug store, in my dreams; she was perfect in every way and I had to find a way to cross the abyss into her world. I thought, "If only I can show her how sensitive I am, tell her about having lived in Germany, let her know that I am really more mature than your average-run-of-the-mill-high-school-sophomore-bore (I mean "boy").

I knew this had to be the first time. You know—love. I knew it because my heart fluttered a little ... temporarily relocated to somewhere near my navel ... and added about forty beats a minute each time I saw her. I would swallow hard and think, "Oh my God ... there she is."

Spending time with her was going to require some very special planning. Some very special thinking. Something probably beyond a male-high-school-sophomore. What could I do?

I thought best on my ten speed bicycle. You know, the kind with a thousand gear sprockets that sparkle in the sunlight as you turn a corner. Mine was neon yellow with racing handle bars, black neoprene grips, racing stirrups, and best of all . . . me—wearing my "coolest" cutoffs, muscle-shirt and Ray·Bans!

I must admit, I did have some pretty great ideas while riding along that day. Then it happened.

While deep in thought about the love of my life, I rode headlong into a car parked at a forty-five-degree angle to the street. I wasn't really hurt, just kind of stunned as I lay out in the back of that '72 El Camino—bike perfectly parallel parked with the rear bumper. Anyone would think I was just getting a tan in the back of Mr. Moore's car. Then I heard it. Laughing. No, cackling. No, guffawing. I looked up, swallowed hard and thought, "oh my God . . . there she is . . . and she saw it all."

But wait, that's not a laugh I hear. It's someone trying to kickstart a '65 Harley. Or is someone nearby just dubbing the mating call of a walrus over a video of the woman I love? I suddenly looked at the woman with whom I was head-over-heels in love and thought, "I think she's going to throw up." How uncouth. How vulgar. How the hell am I ever going to live this down?

I felt the smile begin in my left ear, while my right ear began to spread color across to the other side of my face. I had to admit, it was probably pretty funny. I even laughed myself as I removed myself from Mr. Moore's car and rode off into the sunset. "Besides," I thought, "who could date a girl with a laugh like that?" I realized that French was probably a more suitable language for a man in love anyway.

—Terry Tomlinson,
South Sioux City, NE

New Year's Eve, 1947/48. I'm a high school senior. School party. Big date, with a cute blond I'd dated a few times before. After extensive negotiations with my older brother, I wangle his car for the night. Wash car. Shine shoes. I arrive on the dot at Judy's house. (I'm using real names here: I hope to heck she reads this.)

She's not home. Gone. Split. I've been stood up for a "college man" (I find out later).

Confusion, hurt, anger, in sequence. For about thirty minutes. I go to the party anyway. Meet a REALLY cute blond sophomore I'd not noticed on campus before. Bonnie. Take her home after the party. The long way.

It's now three kids and thirty-seven years later. She says she married me for my last name. Blythe. A better reason than some have, I suppose. Makes her Bonnie Blythe. And she is. Both. Wonderful life. (Wonderful wife.)

Thanks, Judy.

—William Blythe,
Palo Alto, CA

I was about thirty and had just gotten divorced from an abusive husband. wasn't feeling very lovable or attractive at the time. I was on a new teaching job and on my way to work.

I pulled up at a stoplight and a very beautiful gray car pulled up to the right of me. In the car was the most handsome man I have ever seen. . . . no one has ever looked that good.

I looked at him to see if he was going to turn right at the red light. He didn't. He looked back at me and smiled as though looking at me had made his day worthwhile. I was instantly in love with this gorgeous gray haired man but a minute later, he turned right and I turned left. I now knew there was life after divorce even if it was only a minute at a stoplight.

It's been thirteen years now and sometimes I still pass that intersection. Whenever I do, I think of the man who smiled at me. He may never know that he's so highly thought of by someone he only smiled at.

—Rita Conley,
Denver, CO

PERSPECTIVE

I take all these real love stories seriously.

I respect all the love described in these stories.

It's easy to smile at the puppy love story of the eight-year-old who was so desperate to have her love reciprocated that she would threaten violence and suicide. Love me—or I will kill myself and beet you up, she declared. But she wasn't smiling. She hurt. Hers was the unbearably sweet pain of deep longing. Unrequited love arouses desperation. Such feelings shouldn't be dismissed as the cute foolishness of a child. Such feelings are the heart and soul of great literature, high tragedy, and grand opera. The eight-year-old just got an early-warning call from the scary Sphinx that comes bearing two of the Great Mysteries of Life: "How can I love someone so much and they not love me?" and "How can I both love and loathe the same person?"

I laugh and mourn at these stories because I find myself in most of them. Who has not loved too hard too young once—in grade school, high school, or college? My hand isn't raised. I could show you the scars on my soul.

Who does not have a secret love like the man who loves the flower market lady or the woman who still remembers a flashing smile? Me, too—and may those minor romances of my secret life never cease.

And summer love. Oh, to be hit just once more by that kind of electricity!

These memories remind me that my image of self is not progressive, but accumulative. Somewhere in my soul is a boardinghouse full of the people I was once. It came as no surprise to me when psychiatrists discovered multiple personalities. Of course. We all have multiple personalities. When we can't control them, we go crazy. But when we have reasonable dominion over all the dwellers in our boardinghouse of memory, it's called mental health. And most of those residents have love stories to tell.

One of my boarders is a nineteen-year-old cowboy who still works on a ranch in Colorado. It is 1956. He's still disastrously in love with a fifteen-year-old guest at the ranch. She's all he can think about. The sixty-year-old man I am now smiles and says "hormones." Nevertheless, I would live that summer again if I could. Stolen kisses in a coal cellar—dancing every night—howling at the moon. How alive it still seems. Love may not last forever, but love lingers. Lingers so long and hard, as a matter of fact, that I hired a private detective to find my cowboy's long-lost love.

What happened? I'll tell you later.

In the meantime, read some more stories.

Expect the unexpected.

I don't know if this qualifies as a love story or not. It took me a long time to figure out that it does. When I was going through puberty I did what most young boys do. I bought a bunch of very sleazy and much used girlie magazines from an older kid at school and kept them hidden under my mattress where I was sure, of course, that nobody would ever find them.

One day I noticed that several of the magazines were gone, but somebody had replaced them with much newer and higher quality magazines. The girls were much prettier and nicer. I was really excited and really embarrassed. Either my mother or my father or my older sister had done it, because nobody else came into our house. Nobody ever said anything or let on, and I was too scared to ask. This happened every once in awhile for a couple of years, until I left for college. Once there was a whole book about love and sex education with very explicit photographs.

To this day I don't know who tended to my magazine collection. I guess I don't want to know or else I like thinking that any one in my family might have loved me enough to understand my adolescence and not make a fuss about my normal sexuality or embarrass me.

—Jerry,
Port Angeles, WA

On June 21, 1967, I had a blind date with a sailor; I was fifteen and a half and he was two months shy of eighteen. He was my best friend's boyfriend's buddy. They said some girl had just dumped him and he could use a little cheering up.

The meeting was loosely arranged. The actual night of our date, my girlfriend phoned, announcing the guys were at her house and the trio would arrive soon. My parents had just left for their anniversary dinner. They arrived. He took one look at me and decided I was about thirteen. He resorted to playing solitaire in my kitchen since he had no car and I wasn't allowed out without my folks' permission. We played records and I vaguely remember that he did kiss me good-bye. I guess he felt sorry for the poor "kid." When he found out later I was pushing sixteen, he called me for another date.

On Groundhog Day 1969, he left for Viet Nam. Truthfully, I never thought I'd see him again. We finally "consummated" the two-year relationship the night before he left and I got pregnant. He took leave in July, we got married, and my most vivid memory of our wedding day is the fight we had on the way back to my parents' house from the church. When the week's leave was up, I put him on the bus for San Francisco, walked the mile home, and cried all the way, wondering if he would ever return. When he was discharged from the Navy in May of '70, my husband, his alcoholism, our seven-month-old son and I moved from New Jersey to Ohio.

A year later we had a daughter and the family had a new cast member added to the nightmare. His alcoholism and our family violence progressed until 1981 when we hit bottom. We all began 12-step recovery and part two of our marriage unfolded. In a lot of ways, that decade was harder than the first since we had to stop and look our dragons in the eye. That took more courage than letting them chase us. You get used to running from yourself and the adrenaline becomes a new addiction.

But our love is a success story. July 20, 1996 (yes, we got married the same day as the first walk on the moon), we celebrated twenty-seven years of marriage. The statistics say we aren't possible. We definitely screw up the mean on the charts. I'm not real sure why we're still in love and together despite astronomical odds. His name is Roy which means king and mine is Donna which means lady. Lately, I've started thinking of us as a royal couple, deciding we must have an arranged marriage made in heaven that no forces beyond God Himself could destroy. Staying together may not work for everyone. I look back at the years of my life and shudder, wondering where it went. I can't tell you I wouldn't trade some years for happier memories. But I've learned that love is an action verb and neither love nor people nor any relationship is all smooth sailing. Life is bumpy. And I doubt I'd be right here, right now, in the chair next to his, happy, healthy, wealthy and wise if we hadn't grown together all those years. I'm not sorry we stayed married and now I can look forward to our 75th wedding anniversary. We'll be ninety-two and ninety-four that day. Considering how sturdy we apparently are, I bet we'll make it.

—Donna Riddlebarger,
Dayton, OH

I was passing a Thursday evening at Logan International Airport in Boston watching planes take off and land, a hobby in which I partake when I need to ponder life. Looking at the Arrival/Departure schedules and longing to be aboard one of the planes, I caught a glimpse of God or as close a chance as I'll ever get to seeing him. I don't think he realized his omnipotence, which made him even more appealing. As he leisurely made a phone call, I surveyed him in the glass reflection. Dressed in tan Levi Dockers, a white Polo oxford, and a multicolored silk tie, he appeared as though brought to life from a L.L. Bean catalog.

But you may ask what was so special about this man. I will explain it as best I can, but since nobody else can see one's memories, it may be difficult so please bear with me. It was the gentleness about this man which made this longtime skeptic a believer in love at first sight. The way he cradled the phone as though it were a mere six-month-old child, attempting to softly hold its head so that the child wouldn't be harmed, inspired a daydream. I envisioned us at the park in Boston on a cool autumn day, the kind with which New Englanders can readily identify. We were allowing the faint aroma of the ocean to surround us as we relaxed on a checkered picnic blanket. He was cradling me as he had the phone and I'd never felt safer (except for when I was five and my parents let me sleep in their bed, but alas the blissful carefree days of childhood are a distant memory). I was overcome by this feeling of security and could feel myself start to smile amid the wearisome travelers in the airport.

"Flight 476 to Los Angeles is now boarding at Gate 27," the airline announces.

My Adonis replaces the phone with the same tenderness with which he held it and strolls towards the gate without any noticeable alacrity. As I watch this wonderful creature through security, I see the last strands of the sun-streaked golden hair, and a sadness fills me. No, no, not because he is gone, but because he will never *know* of our beautiful picnic in the park.

—Carolyn Byron,
South Boston, MA

In 1912, teenager Louise Groschke met a young church organist named William Britton Wood. They fell in love. By the time Louise was seventeen, she was pregnant with William's child. As soon as her condition became obvious, her stepbrother, Max, who had become head of the family since their father's death, locked Louise in an upstairs bedroom to keep her pregnancy a secret.

William tried to talk to Max to ask for Louise's hand in marriage, but Max would not see William. So, late one night William carried a tall ladder to the Groschke house, propped it under Louise's bedroom window, and quietly helped her out the window and down the ladder to freedom. They were married the next morning and the baby, William George (my father), was born one month later. Over the years, Louise and William had twelve more children and a long and happy marriage.

—Becky Britton Wood,
Seattle, WA

This is a love story about how pajamas made me lose and find my mind.

I have reached the age (70) where I begin to wonder about what ever happened to people I knew when I was young. There was one special girl I met at a USO dance when I was in the Navy. We had a one-week love affair I have never forgotten, but I was shipped out before I could tell her I was leaving and we lost touch. After the war, I married someone else, had kids, a career and all those things.

Well, I wanted to find out about this girl. So I hired a private investigator to look for her and he found her. She was living in Palm Springs and since I live in Los Angeles, I thought I would just call her up and go see her. She was really glad to hear from me, especially after I explained why I had disappeared. So I went to see her. We had a wonderful time. And it felt like we were kids again. She was just as attractive to me as I was to her.

She said that life was short and we ought to spend a weekend together like old times. I went back home with fire in my heart. When I looked at myself in the mirror, I didn't look so good. If I was going to spend a romantic weekend, I would need to have some decent covering. I'm an old man with old man's habits, and I have always slept naked and slopped around the house in an old pair of house slippers and a bathrobe I've had forever. My wife doesn't care, but I couldn't go to Palm Springs with these things.

I went down to the store and bought two pairs of nice pajamas, a silk bathrobe, and some new house slippers. I got some new underwear and socks, too. When I got home, I thought my wife was over at her sister's house, so I went in and was just unwrapping my new stuff when my wife walked in. She was really pleased because she was tired of the way I dressed for bed. Now I had to lie to her about why I had them and wear my new stuff at home. I felt awful.

I have never worn pajamas and am not used to them. That night when I was trying to put them on, I got one leg in and the other leg stuck in the waistband and hopped around until I lost my balance and fell backwards in the bathroom and hit my head, knocking myself cuckoo. I cut my head and got a concussion.

The next thing I knew I woke up in the hospital and I couldn't remember why.

My wife brought me several new nightshirts to replace my pajamas, but I couldn't remember why I had pajamas in the first place. Slowly it all came back to me. I called my old girlfriend to explain, but she didn't believe me. She said it was the last time I was ever going to stand her up and slammed down the phone. It's just as well. I'm getting used to sleeping in night shirts. Old love and new pajamas are dangerous.

—*Anonymous*

I was a high school junior in a suburb of Cleveland in 1964–65 when I met the very lovely and pleasant Brenda Andrews in art class. We shared small talk, humor, attitudes and an obvious enjoyment of each other's company. In fact, I soon was certain that I wanted her to be my girl. So the next step was to ask her out, right?

Wrong! I'm Caucasian and Brenda is Afro-American (colored or Negro in those days) and in mid-sixties suburban America, race-mixing was absolutely, positively not done. It could be harmful to one's physical, emotional and social well being, and sad to say, I didn't have the courage to buck society at that time. So Brenda and I remained friends till we graduated and then I never saw her again.

Since then I've thought about her often and always believed that she shared my feelings and may have felt as helpless as I about our impossible situation. I used to resent society for placing us in that position and wished I could see Brenda again and complete our story by telling her how I felt. I long ago ditched those feelings, but people are constantly feeling trapped by various prejudices and my story might convince some of them to follow their hearts.

—Percy Hilo,
Seattle, WA

PERSPECTIVE

Pain.

There is a lot of pain in these true love stories.

Love causes pain. Love cures pain. And love is a pain.

Where love is, pain is never far away. Love will fill your heart, break your heart, and heal the heart that's broken. And it is true that every love story has an unhappy ending, sooner or later—even if the love lasts a lifetime, somebody dies first, leaving somebody behind with the pain of grief.

Love is blind—and love opens eyes.

Falling in love with someone of another race, another religion, or another class will be both painful and instructive, sooner or later. Falling in love with someone not of your sexual persuasion will bring pain and knowledge, sooner or later. And falling in love with love instead of a person will pain you and teach you. Sooner or later. Love is an active verb—a river, not a pond.

Love can make you want to die—and love can make you want to live.

You are about to read a classic story—a romantic story—a script for a film. For all the love that's in it, don't skip over the pain. The smell of burning flesh is in it as well as the heat of the burning heart. Hemingway's novel A Farewell to Arms *is about such a love, but he made it up. This story is, in its own way, about a farewell to hands. Two people lived through this. The pain and the love are true.*

I was the navigator on a B-24 Liberator four-engine bomber that crashed at March Field, Riverside, California on February 1, 1944. I was trapped under the top gun turret in the burning wreckage. After it burned a while, the turret shifted and I was able to wiggle on my back to a rupture in the side of the aircraft where I was pulled on out by a couple of infantry men.

I was taken to the station hospital where my diagnosis read: Burns, second degree, face and neck: Burns, third degree, right arm, right hand, left hand, right thigh, right leg, right foot, left knee. Shock, systemic, due to burns.

The burns were debrided and dressed and my left hand was amputated. When I was ready for transfer to a plastic surgery center I was sent to Bushnell General Hospital in Brigham City, Utah. Normally they sent you to the center nearest your home which should have been Walter Reed Hospital in Washington, D.C., but my physical condition had deteriorated to the point that I couldn't survive the trip to D.C.

At Bushnell, my right hand was amputated and I survived thirteen skin graft operations and my spirits were very low. Then in July the Army initiated a Cadet Nurse program wherein they brought senior student nurses to Bushnell to complete their training and prepare them for positions in the Army Nurse Corps.

My whole outlook on life abruptly changed one morning when two nurses entered my room. One was a Major, the hospital's chief nurse; the other was a cadet nurse. The Major said, "Lt. Rawley, this is Miss Kay. She is going to be taking care of you."

Although I had not been displaying much interest in what was going on around me, my interest in life suddenly skyrocketed. There before me stood a young lady who sparked more interest in me than any girl I had ever seen.

This tall, slim cadet nurse had lovely dark brown hair, dark brown eyebrows and beautiful sparkling green eyes. She had a light sprinkling of freckles across the bridge of her nose and a cute crooked smile that lit up her whole face.

I forgot the loss of my hands as I watched the pretty nurse go efficiently about her chores. I used every excuse I could invent to increase the number of her visits to my room. We became very good friends, but eventually she finished her training, left Bushnell, and became a lieutenant in the Army Nurse Corps.

We kept in touch with each other and after fourteen months of hospitalization I was ready to be released from the hospital and sent back home to Northern New York never to see her again. But wait, because I had apparently gained sufficient proficiency with my artificial limbs, I was asked by the Air Force to return to duty as a hospital liaison officer for the purpose of traveling to the various military hospitals in the U.S. to talk to and encourage new arm amputees.

I was permitted to set my own itinerary, so wherever Lt. Kay was stationed or transferred to, I just happened to show up there. Our courtship continued until WWII ended. We were married on June 26, 1946, in a military wedding in the little chapel at Fort Douglas, in Salt Lake City, Utah.

The chief nurse at Bushnell didn't know how right she was when she said that Miss Kay was going to be taking care of me. She is still doing so after fifty years. Because I was sent to Bushnell instead of Walter Reed, I found my wonderful eternal companion who inspired me to go on and obtain BS and MS degrees in wildlife management and complete a thirty-four-year career with Utah's Division of Wildlife Resources winding up as Chief of Planning and Programming.

—Edwin Rawley,
Bountiful, UT

He stood to the left of me high in the bleachers, a mellow baritone voice buried in the bass section. I have always loved bass sections . . . tall, strong hunks of men with deep, rich voices booming over the sopranos. He was all of that and more. He had a boyish Norwegian face, light complexion, blue eyes and beautifully combed mop of blond thick hair. But even more than that. He had the most beautiful voice I had ever heard. He was Nelson Eddy and Rudolph Valentino rolled into one. And even more than that. He sang solos and I sang solos and once in a while we would sing duets and our voices made love together. I fantasized myself as Jeanette MacDonald in the arms of her beloved Eddy. We never talked much . . . just sang.

The results were more beautiful than any spoken word. My secret romance burst into flame when at last near the end of that college year he asked for a date. Just a quiet evening driving around in his new 1950 Olds. Drove into the country and parked by the railroad tracks to watch for a train to come by which never did. We necked up a storm. Never said much—just necked. The longer we waited for the train, the more we necked and the less we said. Our departure had even less words. A few days later the choir rehearsed for the last time before summer break. We never saw each other again.

Forty years later and two thousand miles from that small college campus in Indiana, the telephone rang. He was calling from California. He tracked me through the alumni office. His first question: "Do you still sing?" "You bet I do!" I have a feeling that our voices are still in love with each other.

—Marian Yunghans,
Bellingham, WA

I was sweaty, exhausted, and thirsty from a demanding performance at the junior college I attended, so I stopped for a drink at the water fountain in the hall. When I stood up I bumped into an incredibly handsome young man, with sky blue eyes.

Instantly, I regretted having washed off the stage makeup. My coloring is not what one would call "dramatic." It's more like a freshly washed sheet.

"Are you the young lady who sang in the show?"

Good grief! His voice matched his looks—deep, resonant, rumbling even!

Somehow I managed to gasp out one word, "Yes."

"It was magnificent—and like casting pearls before swine."

No one had ever spoken to me like that—ever!

I was all of sixteen years old, immersed in studying opera and the essential voice lessons required for the art. I was convinced that I was painfully "plain," that handsome boys weren't interested in me, etc., etc. Nevertheless, this blond Greek god asked for my phone number and permission to call me "one day soon."

He did call. And so began some of the most marvelous years of my young life. I was undeterred by warnings from "the girls," who claimed that he was a bounder and a cad. He attended all my performances and looked for excuses for me to sing. We were "the perfect pair." We liked the same things. We did everything together.

He made me beautiful.

Months went by in a dreamlike haze, but I couldn't forget the girls' warnings. One night I finally could not contain myself any longer. Through a series of bumbling attempts, I managed to ask him if what they said was true.

He pulled over to the curb of the tree-lined street. My first thought was "This is it. He's either going to say 'we're all done,' or do something drastic!" I had terrified myself!

Neither of those things happened.

He put the car in neutral, engaged the emergency brake and, with motor still running and lights till on, turned to face me.

"That was different. I didn't love them."

Then he turned back, released the brake, put the car in gear and drove me home.

I didn't touch ground for months!

The following school year he transferred to the Pasadena Playhouse. For most of the year, we saw one another several times every week. But, when spring came, he called less and less. I had no formal claim on him and, in those days, girls didn't call boys. So I waited.

The other boys seemed so dull. I had my "dancing buddy," my "theater buddy," my "opera buddy," etc., and once in a while one would want to be more than "buddies." On those few occasions, I tried to sidestep as tactfully as possible.

The next year he went into the armed services, choosing the navy over being drafted into the army. Before he left, he said all the right things, made all the proper promises, and I settled in to wait some more.

After boot camp, he had occasional leaves. He called the week prior to my twentieth birthday, just before I was moving to Santa Barbara to finish my last year at the University of California. In a very serious tone, he explained that he *had* to see me before I left—that we were going to spend the entire day and evening together. Of course, I made that space in my life for him.

We did spend the day together, laughing,

exploring, eating, then off to see *The Corn Is Green* at the Player's Ring Theater in Hollywood. A perfect day. I was convinced that it would not end without a "significant" event. Although I had a hard time admitting it, even to myself, I was hoping that he would formally ask me to marry him.

That is not what happened.

Instead of driving directly to my house, he drove to a secluded spot, turned off the lights and the engine. My heart was dancing!

"There is something I must tell you," he began.

I can't remember the rest of the words. I can't remember much except shock—then disbelief—then numbness.

"You prefer . . . boys?"

What did that mean?

Not my knight in shining armor!

This was not happening!

Then more words, something like, "We'll always be special to one another . . . I do love you . . . we are family . . ." and on and on and on.

I just sat and waited.

Finally, he asked, "Do you understand?"

How could I respond to such a stupid question? What could I say? I just nodded—and tried to keep my eyes from leaking.

We drove home. I don't know how I got into the house. I remember trying to feel NOTHING—refusing to allow tears—treasuring the emptiness of numbness.

When I arrived at my college housing, his letter was waiting for me. I saved it for years—a gentle, loving plea for understanding and a pledge of "forever love." Then I cried—a lot!

As I write this, I am sixty-one years old. I've continued to do theater through the years. Forty years ago I married a gentle, charming, intelligent, devoted man. We have three adult daughters with their own families. We've managed forty years of tragedies and triumphs and are beginning to think of how to manage what we hope will be our "golden years."

Still, the memory lingers—even though I finally threw away the letter—even gave away the gifts of jewelry and such that my "first love" gave to me. We've lost track of one another.

But, now and again, I do wonder about him and hope that he's had a rewarding worthwhile life and that he's happy with himself.

Mostly, I remember being beautiful.

—Claire Hodgin,
Scotts Valley, CA

This is an innocent erotic love story. Early one morning while our husbands slept, a friend and I were combing the outdoor market in New Orleans looking for some unusual things to take home to our sons—two mothers on a mission. When we reached for an exotic African percussion instrument at the same time, her hand brushed my forearm. She gasped and said, "You have the softest skin I've ever felt in my life. May I touch your face and neck?"

"Sure," I said, expecting her to ask me about beauty products. But she surprised me.

"Now I know how a man feels when he touches a woman."

It was a lovely moment—a random experience of great sweetness.

—*Anonymous*

We, my wife and I, have this country house and yard. It's both a necessity and a luxury. Living scarcely 47 paces from the church and office, we need a place that's away, separate. So we have this place, we call it "Wellspring," seventy-five miles away. It's also extravagant, not in dollars so much but in emotions. We luxuriate in the yard and woods. We meditate by the stream. We make love better there than anywhere else.

On Mondays I usually take a big bite out of the day to travel there and work at restoring this old place—replacement windows, new siding, paint and caulking. I leave early, as in before dawn, and stay late, leaving only enough daylight to stop and fly fish a favorite pool on the Redbank.

It was on one of those Monday workdays that I fell in love. The state road runs through and over the rolling hills of western Pennsylvania. The commonwealth has taken to widening and flattening the roadway, something of an environmental heresy. They have to manage the traffic at the work site. That's where I met her. She was holding the "Slow" on one side; "Stop" on the other side sign, with a walkie-talkie strapped on the pole. She was dressed like the men who drove large earth-movers, put backs into shovel motions, and swung large hammers—blue jeans, orange vest over a tee shirt, hard hat and work boots. But her profile was different. No bulging midriff here, not even a muscled arm. This construction worker was thin and trim and shapely, with the kind of figure that attracts most men who are still wired for action if not fantasy.

Every Monday morning—rain or shine—she was there—"Slow" or "Stop." I always hoped for "Stop" so I could pause and reflect upon the contours the state was taking away and giving, if only for a few minutes. Once I even slowed so she'd give me a "Stop" when I probably could have made "Slow." Each time I came I waved and she waved back—one of those feminine waves where the fingers undulate and make a clear distinction from the two-fingered salute type men give. You don't suppose she waved only at me—on Mondays!? Probably not.

Then one day that stretch of the roadway was finished and she was gone, to direct traffic somewhere else or laid off for the winter. I miss her and our brief Monday love affairs. But there's more work to be done just a bit south, and the warmer days of spring are near.

—Robert Rigg,
Mars, PA

The big band era was an exciting time in America. Live music and dancing was the fashion. As a young woman, I loved to dance. Along with my three sisters and my neighborhood girlfriends, we could be found at the Trianon Ball Room on Saturday nights.

I could waltz, two-step, jitterbug, polka, and schottische. During the summer, we would go to the lakes to dance for they would always have live music.

One particular evening, a man asked me to dance. He was pleasant but not an extraordinary dancer and he talked all the time. Little did I know then, what an impact he would have on my life.

We danced the fox-trot and then came a jitter-bug rhythm and he still would use the same old steps. This annoyed me. As the dance ended, he deposited me next to my sister and asked us if we would like a soft drink. "Sure," she said. As we finished our drink, he reached over and took my hand and led me out onto the dance floor, same old two-step again.

When we had completed our dance, I excused myself and headed for the ladies lounge. I wasted time there. By now he would surely have another partner. I strolled out and there he was! . . . HORRORS . . . I thought, he is like glue to wallpaper, and couldn't seem to get rid of him.

We danced the last dance and he asked to take me home. "No!" I said. "My father's rules are my sister and I go together, my sister and I come home together." "May I have your phone number?" he asked. "All right." At least over the phone I could say no.

He never called me.

The following Sunday, I took the bus to see a girlfriend who lived on Alki Avenue and I had to transfer to another bus. While I waited at the bus stop, he drove up in a new car and opened the passenger door and said, "Hi!, get in."

"No, I am waiting for my bus."

The bus approached and stopped behind him while he just sat. The bus driver honked and he still just sat. It didn't appear that he would ever move so I jumped into the car.

We drove off around Alki beach and talked and then I said, "That green house is where my friend lives and I get off." He drove past the house and kept on going. I yelled "Let me out!!" Panic stricken, I fumbled to find the door handle.

"All right! Did I miss your stop?" he calmly replied. He made a U turn and stopped at her door.

"How did you find me?" I asked him. "I went to your house and visited with your father, he told me where you would be."

Often he would phone and say, "Pat, I want to go to the movies." I would yell, "NO!" and a half hour later he would be at my door.

Sometimes there were long hesitations over the phone before he announced his message. What an unusual person I thought, but my family adored him, especially my father and brother.

When my brother bought his first car and took him for a ride, the faulty wiring burned up. He was there to help him repair it and teach him mechanics.

Two months had gone by before he told me he was stone deaf and had been educated at the Iowa State School for the Deaf. He relied on lip reading and was very proficient at it. He could talk and also used sign language to communicate.

After I realized the problem, I learned to cope. We never talked to each other over the phone, or in the dark, and I learned to face him when speaking. He was always such a happy person and very good for my personality.

We often went dancing and I even taught him a few new steps. What I didn't realize was that I was falling in love with that big Dane from Iowa.

Six months later, he asked me to marry him and gave me a beautiful diamond ring.

We were married in Seattle and had a happy marriage for forty-three years.

—Patricia Jensen,
Seattle, WA

PERSPECTIVE

Have you noticed the part incredible coincidence and dumb luck play in these stories? It's certainly true in my own love story. I met my wife almost twenty-five years ago in a garden in Japan. We figure that we had a window of opportunity of about thirty seconds and would never ever have crossed paths again.

A young friend frets over her lack of luck—feeling that Mr. Right and she must have missed each other somewhere along the line by the same thirty seconds. She wishes she could rewind the film of her life and take a closer look at who was in some of the scenes with her.

When I read the personal ads in newspapers I'm drawn to the section where people are trying to rescue luck—trying to find someone they saw only briefly. I quote only one:

Tall red-headed woman in dark green dress—last Friday. You were getting on the Vashon ferry and I was coming off. Our eyes locked. We passed. When I looked back, you looked back. When I parked my motorcycle and came back to try to get on the ferry to find you, it was too late. You waved to me from the deck as the ferry pulled out. I must find you—we may be each other's destiny. Call Trevor at———. If anybody can help me, please call.

Trevor is going crazy by now. He doesn't even describe himself. He just knows she knows. The longer he thinks about her the more wonderful she becomes. And the tall red-headed woman in the dark green dress? I'd like to know what she thought and felt. I'd like to know the rest of the story.

That's true for most of the real-life stories in this book. When you finish, the question hangs there: And then what happened? Where are they now? We know the story told by the lover, but how would the lovee tell the story? What one person might describe as the near-miss of a great love another person might call a close escape from a fate worse than death. Anybody who gets fixed up with an absolutely-can't-miss-perfect-blind-date by a friend knows the paradox.

Love is never final—there's always a sequel or the hope for one.

Margery and I were childhood sweethearts dating off-and-on from the time we were thirteen until about age twenty. We were pretty serious about each other. We graduated from high school and our lives changed and separated. She went east to Connecticut and then to college in New Mexico. I went to Ohio, then Hawaii. In time we would marry different people although I would also always consider her my first and strongest love.

Some fifteen years later (about 1978) my life was a mess. Not the sort of life one would deliberately set out to create.

I was suffering from chronic alcohol abuse, a

disease which runs in my family. I nearly died from withdrawals and subsequently committed myself to a hospital.

Upon release from the hospital three weeks later, I was physically, emotionally and financially bankrupt. I had no idea what would become of my life.

In short order, I would legally divorce and take custody of two sons aged nine and ten. I would strike off into single parenthood vowing never again to marry.

Several weeks after being released form the hospital, I was sitting around with my mother one evening reviewing a box of family photos. I came across a picture of me and my childhood sweetheart taken before a school dance. We were about seventeen and deeply in love at the time.

I said, "God, why did I have to have that eleven-year marriage. What a disaster. Why couldn't I have married Margery and lived a more normal life instead. I loved her so much. It never even occurred to me to ask her to marry. Why did I have to go through that other marriage: Why did I have to go through all that other stuff?

"I think I will try to find her," I said to my mother. My mother said, "Maybe you'd better go back to the hospital for awhile. You're not even finished with the divorce you're going through. This is not the time to be thinking about another relationship.

"Besides that," she added, "you haven't seen nor talked to Margery for how long—fifteen years? She's probably happily married, has four children and lives in New Mexico. Forget her and just concentrate on raising those darling boys."

I reached for the South Bay telephone directory and began looking up people by Margery's maiden name, Southworth. There were a dozen or so of them in the Los Angeles area. I began telephoning them to see if maybe, just maybe I might reach a sister or aunt or someone who might know where she was. I felt very, very strongly about this—compelled to act.

I did not reach her or a relative that night but

I reaffirmed to my mother how strongly I felt that I would be seeing her again.

The next morning I left Rolling Hills at 7:30 a.m. to cross the Los Angeles basin for Hollywood, where I worked. For no apparent reason I decided to go a different way. I took a left, I headed for the San Diego Freeway, a direction I seldom went since it was a long way to get to work.

As I approached the freeway (along with millions of other commuters), I was stopped by the red light that meters people onto the freeway system there. I waited for the light to change to green.

While I was waiting a tan van pulled up alongside me and began honking. I couldn't quite see up into the van, but I could tell there was a person with large dark glasses driving.

She raised her dark glasses up over her forehead and it was her! Margery Southworth! I was stunned. I put my forehead on the steering wheel and began to cry. Then I started to laugh, I just couldn't believe it. The light changed and I had to get on the freeway. I stayed in the right lane and put on my right blinker to get off the freeway. She responded. We were still communicating, I thought.

We left the freeway and pulled into the parking lot of Mattel Toys. I got out of my car, walked over to her and we gave each other a big hug. We talked and asked each other a few questions (she had been single for fourteen years). I asked for her phone number. Later in the day, I called her and we made arrangements to have dinner the following Friday night.

Eight months later we had a large wedding on a hilltop overlooking our elementary school and Los Angeles. Sixteen years later we are still happily married living in the Federal Way area.

We have both accepted this relationship as a gift, a very special gift from God. A miracle.

—Patrick Godfrey,
Federal Way, WA

This is really my mother's love story. I asked her to tell you, but she's too shy. It's too good not to pass on. It explains why my brother and I say we owe our existence to peanuts.

When she graduated from high school my mother had everything going for her but one. She was pretty, smart, and came from a well-to-do family, but she was terminally shy, especially around men. Boys didn't like to take her out because she was so quiet. She went off to the same college her mother went to and to please her mother, she agreed to be rushed by her mother's sorority. At the first rush party, she sat out of sight at one end of a room, in a corner by a table that had snacks on it. She ate a lot of peanuts out of nervousness.

She began to notice a waiter, who seemed to be as shy as she. He never said anything, but he was taking care of her. He kept her glass filled with nonalcoholic punch and he kept her peanut bowl full. From time to time their eyes met and they smiled at each other.

When the dancing started and the party got rowdy, she walked into the kitchen and out the back door to escape. As she was going down the alley, she heard someone calling, "Wait, wait, please wait." It was the waiter, running down the alley after her with a paper bag in his hands. They stood in awkward silence, just smiling. Then he reached into the bag, pulled out a whole can of peanuts and offered them to her and said, "I only wish these were pearls."

He ran back up the alley and into the sorority house.

Well, one thing led to another.

Twenty-five years later, on the silver wedding anniversary of my mother and the waiter (my father), he gave her a sterling silver jar marked "peanuts." She thought that was the gift and was really pleased. But there was more. When she lifted the lid, inside was a string of pearls.

No gift ever pleased her more. She wore those pearls as her only jewelry for years. When my father was killed in a traffic accident, she put the silver peanut can in his coffin with him. I've never seen her wear the pearls since. I think I know where they are, but I'm too shy to ask.

—Marilyn, Tacoma, WA

We need to head back to the fall of '85. I was twenty-five and working as a systems analyst for a large financial institution in Pittsburgh. But that's not important. What is important is that I was walking to work one morning after a night of rain. The sidewalks were still puddled and the air was cool. A relatively nice morning even though I was walking through the middle of a city. As in the habit of most commuters (and to keep my shoes dry) I was walking head down with my eyes just far enough ahead to keep from walking into anyone. So I suppose it was no surprise that her shoes were the first thing to catch my attention.

The shoes were attractive enough (as shoes go) and as we continued to walk toward each other her ankles soon followed into my line of sight. They, too, were attractive and as we continued to get closer I continued to slowly tilt my head up to allow her to slide into view. If I may borrow one of your own phrases "it's enough to say she was lovely." She was dressed professionally and was obviously on her way to an office as was I, albeit in opposite directions.

Anyway, as we drew closer my eyes came up to see the rest of her and when my eyes got as high as her face I realized I was caught. I did not see the attractive but downturned face I expected. Instead I found myself looking eye to eye with her. Caught red handed (eyed?). Apparently she had been watching me watch her. I was preparing to be terribly embarrassed and receive the look reserved for leches and people who refuse to forget that professional women are still at the heart of it women, when, much to my surprise she smiled. And such a warm smile it was too that all I could do was smile back. She gave me a smile that said she was glad the extra time she took in the morning to look her best was worth it. A smile that said that she too didn't forget that profession aside, she was a woman at the heart of it all. A smile that said thank you to an unspoken compliment. It was a smile that made me forget where I was and why I was there. It lifted my heart above the concrete to where skies are always blue.

She smiled, I smiled, we passed and I have never seen her again. Eleven years later, I still think of her and smile. I hope she still thinks of me.

—Chip Galusha,
Farmville, NC

A very old man—George—who had been placed in a nursing home by his family was a sad case—nobody ever came to see him. One day he stopped talking and refused to leave his room. He was cooperative enough with the staff and functional enough to take care of himself. He continued to eat and bathe. But he became a mute recluse, sitting alone in his room in his rocking chair all day staring out the window. The staff decided he had a right to live as he wished, so they let him be.

A woman resident—Maggie—had taken an interest in George, and when he disappeared she went in to visit with him. He didn't seem to mind, but he didn't respond, either. She had started working on a quilt and over time she moved her handiwork little by little into his room. She spent her days sewing and telling her life story, while he sat staring out the window. She had been in vaudeville. She had a million stories and was very happy to have someone listen to her. Nobody knew what he thought. He sat and stared. She talked. Months went by.

When Maggie finished the quilt, it was put on display in the main lobby of the nursing home. Everyone said it was one of the most beautiful quilts they ever saw. She was especially proud since it was the only quilt she had ever made.

The same week the quilt was finished, George passed away.

In the drawer of his nightstand the staff found an envelope marked, "To be opened when I die." The note inside said only, "Tell Maggie I love her." When they told her, she cried as if her heart would break. She had loved him, too. She had made the quilt just for him.

And that's why George was buried wrapped in Maggie's quilt.

—as told to R. F.

I am thirteen years old and the middle child of three girls in my family. When I was around eight, our family became good friends with an English family with three boys all similar in ages to my sisters and me. While the friendship between our parents grew, the friendship between all us kids grew even faster. Some of my favorite childhood memories are of the six of us running around outside at midnight playing "Ghost in the Graveyard." The object of the game is to venture out into the darkness looking for the one who was hiding. Once you saw this person you screamed "squished bananas" and ran back to base before you got caught. Anyway, we all got together and had the best time playing this wonderful game.

While I was close to all three of the boys and their parents, I especially took a liking to the eldest, who is a year and a half older than me. I grew very close to him and developed a huge crush on him. By then, I had turned eleven. Then, one day they had to tell us some awful news—they were moving to France. I was devastated. My best friends were moving to France and I'd probably never see them again.

They've been gone for five years now and we still keep in touch. They've come over almost every summer to visit us and every time I see him I fall deeper in love. My family chides me for they don't think I know what it feels like to be in love since I have never had a deep relationship before. But every time I see him and look into his eyes, I know it has to be. I can't explain what I feel, but it's something that won't go away.

We have such a wonderful friendship, something that I value more than anything. I just wish somehow we could go further with that.

I saw him a month ago. He and his brothers came and stayed for a week. We had the best times together. We even played Ghost in the Graveyard and had as much fun as we did when we were young. I have never outwardly told Jason how I feel about him, but I think he knows. I miss him so much. Every morning I wake up and wonder what he is doing in England, where they now live. He is so special to me and I hope someday, somewhere, we can be together.

—Dana Waesche,
Westport, CT

I had been married about nine years when I had an affair with another woman. One day I got a "mash" note at my office. It came in the mail, with no return address. The woman said she saw me almost every day and had fallen in love with me. She thought I was attractive and she especially liked the way I was considerate of other people. She was right about that last part. I do have good manners. The letters came about once a week for a while. I liked the way she wrote and I was relieved that she didn't seem to want anything from me. She never asked to meet me and never asked me to write her back. Sometimes she sent poetry.

The mail began to affect me. I looked in the mirror and saw that I wasn't in great shape, so I started to work out at a gym. I went and bought some new clothes, which is something I don't often do. She noticed. She wrote me that I was looking healthy and she liked my new style. She even sent me a great tie.

The bad thing was that I felt guilty. I love my wife and we have a workable marriage that is in about the standard condition after nine years. I have never strayed, but I've thought about it, like most guys do. It really became a problem when my anonymous admirer started sending me erotic mail. Nothing dirty or pornographic, just short stories and some photographs of men and women kissing. I liked it. But I felt guilty because I was beginning to look for this woman everywhere I went.

Months went by. One day I got a book in the mail. *Sensual Love for Sensual Couples*. It was full of pictures of couples making love in every place but bed—on tables, in hot tubs, and on and on. Rubbing and sucking and licking and fondling. Using oil and perfume and birch branches. It drove me crazy. Her letters talked about how she wanted to do these things with me. I confess I wanted to do those things with her.

Well, by now I am in good shape, well-dressed and eager for love and sex.

One day a huge bouquet of yellow roses arrived at my office. There was a note enclosed that said she had decided to take the chance of meeting me and asked me to meet her in the lobby of a nearby hotel that very afternoon. She would be wearing a yellow rose, sitting in the main lobby.

I went out of my mind. I couldn't go, but I wanted to go, and I had to go.

But I thought I would check her out first. I went to the hotel, went in through a side door, and went up the stairs to the mezzanine where there is a balcony that overlooks the lobby.

And there she was. Beautifully dressed. Wearing a yellow rose. Sitting on a couch all alone in the middle of the lobby. It was my wife. It was our tenth wedding anniversary.

—*Anonymous*

My mother is forty-five and I'm twenty-five. She and my dad met and married and had me while they were still in college, and as far as I know, they've had a good marriage and a good life.

When she was going back to her twenty-fifth high school reunion a couple of years ago, she got out her high school yearbook and all her keepsakes from those years and showed them to me. I was amazed to see how much my mom and I looked alike at the same age. We went through the whole yearbook. When she came to one boy's picture, she began to cry.

The boy's name was Benny, and she went steady with him for three years. They were madly in love, but her parents and his parents were against the relationship because he was Jewish and her parents were Baptists. Benny and my mom wanted to run away together or elope and get married or at least go to the same college. Their parents arranged things so they would go to colleges on the opposite side of the country. Benny and my mom tried to keep things going, but it didn't work. Mom fell in love with my dad, and Benny went to medical school and became a flight surgeon in the air force.

They met again at the reunion. I don't know what happened. My mom didn't talk about how she felt about seeing him. But I did find out he wasn't married. About a year ago, my mom gave a dinner party and invited me to come and meet some old friends of hers from high school days. When I walked into the living room, I saw one of the most attractive men I've ever seen. Truly tall, dark, and handsome. He was introduced to me as Dr. Benjamin ——.

He was my mom's Benny. And it was love at first sight for him and me.

To make a long story short, we had a wonderful romance. We kept it a secret at first. It seemed such a crazy thing. We even went to see a psychologist and a marriage counselor. I wanted to make sure it was really me he loved and not my mom. Finally, we decided to get married. We told his parents first, and they said it was fate. When we told mom, she cried and got hysterical and then she laughed. I think both she and my dad are relieved at the way things turned out.

We got married two months ago. So far, so good. Only time will tell if we did the right thing, but that's true of any marriage. He may have been my mom's Benny once, but he's my Benny now.

—S. F. G., Louisville, KY

PERSPECTIVE

Falling in love with your mom's old boyfriend and marrying him?

That's weird. That's really weird.

I would be surprised if you didn't think that at least a couple of times while reading these stories. I did. Though I bet if we compared stories, we wouldn't be talking about the same ones. I think what we mean by "weird" is that we wouldn't do something like that or that's not love to us. Or else it's weird because we've added our imagination to the story—details and motives and reactions—that are not really in the story as written but in our minds as readers. The story isn't weird, we are.

A psychiatrist once told me that if we knew exactly what went on in the minds of the apparently normal people around us all the time we would run for our lives. Or if our friends and families knew what happened in our own secret minds, they would have us arrested. But when we're in control of our weirdness and it works in our favor, that makes us at least appear normal.

Recently I went to a Friday evening Big Band Dance in Seattle. Hundreds of couples waltzing and two-stepping and fox-trotting around. Tall blond stick of a woman dancing up close and tight with a huge fat guy with tattooed bald head and a bushy beard. Weird. Across the floor, an ancient couple—Asian—dressed almost exactly alike in khaki pants, plaid shirts, and tennis shoes—wrapped in each other's arms like vines—not dancing, just swaying to the music. Weird. Beyond them, a flashy young woman dancing like she was in a chorus line, while her dull little man stood in one place like a ship anchored in a storm. She kissed him between pirouettes. He just grinned and held on. Weird. Everywhere—weird love.

There were no glamorous couples—no perfect matches—but so what?

You want my opinion? We're all a little weird. And life is a little weird. And when we find someone whose weirdness is compatible with ours, we join up with them and fall into mutually satisfying weirdness—and call it love—true love.

He was 5'9", slim, with a Tommy Lee Jones smile and big brown eyes sparkling with intelligence and humor under eyelashes so long and thick and dark they could have been store-bought. He was so fascinated by my mind and the unusual nature of my character that he REALLY DIDN'T CARE that I was fat and plain. He devoured my prose, he'd pause to comment, so impressed that his eyes would water up—then he'd start hollering that I should be making at least a perfunctory effort to get published. He was Peter O'Toole with a southern accent and a double dose of testosterone.

At the time, my mother, best friend/worst enemy, light and power of my life was dying. One day I just lost my mind and had my daughter Christie tell him I had left for Cincinnati to marry a policeman. There was no policeman. It was a ploy. Madness.

If you should see Danny O'Neal, please tell him this: My mother died September 17, 1990. I have recovered from it. There is still no cop in Cincinnati. I am still single. I am saner. All men still pale in comparison to Danny. I'd like to see him just one more time. To start over or to get over . . . either would be nice.

—Lilly McLain,
Ft. Smith, OK

It was over four years ago that I invited my mother for a visit (she loved to travel), knowing that my eighty-three-year-old father would no longer agree to travel anywhere from their California home. But she declined kindly, saying, "No, he would never leave me." How prophetic those words.

It was only a few months later when my mother was devastated by a severe stroke, leaving her paralyzed, unable to speak, not responsive to our questions, but usually aware of my sister's and my visits and most especially of my Dad. She now smiles at us when we arrive and often during visits and sometimes at our little jokes and family stories. But, she is unable to in any way care for herself and has been in a nursing home ever since the stroke.

And so has my father—not as a resident there, but as a daily, without fail, visitor. Most of every day he is there—feeding her, massaging her wasted muscles, reading to her, telling her of any news from distant friends and family, giving her back rubs, singing little songs, showing her family photo albums, watching over her in every way he can to help her be more comfortable.

My Dad is eighty-eight now and he has become a legend in the nursing home because of his devotion. He has been with my mother every day since that terrible evening—the night of their 59th wedding anniversary. . . . She knows (you can tell from the way she looks at him) that he would never leave her—as she wasn't willing to leave him either, even for a short family visit.

So, this is what my Dad, Raymond Doyen, has taught me about devotion and caring and compassion and love and duty—and he has never been one to give advice . . . only the example of his life.

—Anne Joeri Doyen Perrin,
Corona de Tucson, AZ

I am fifty-six, a judge, happily married thirty years with six kids (twenty-nine to seven). But for a few minutes this morning, I was twenty, in the air force in Germany, and visiting the 1958 World's Fair in Brussels, Belgium. Thanks to your *Uh-Oh*, page 67.

Amid the crowds of people at the fair, and from a distance of about fifty feet, there walked a girl about fifteen or sixteen, five foot one inches, one hundred lbs., waist length brown hair in a pony tail and matching brown eyes. She was one of a class of girls in school uniform, supervised by an aging and stern nun. The girl and I made eye contact, and I followed that group and that girl for about an hour, to the chagrin and displeasure of my traveling companion, who was not willing to accept my stricken heart as valid.

I never got closer than twenty feet of her, but will forever remember one lingering look between us over a small reflecting pool and fountain, in Brussels, Belgium, in the summer of 1958.

—Jim Wright,
Long Beach, CA

I was going through a rather devastating divorce. Shortly after I moved out of the apartment I had shared with my husband, I started seeing a man named Barry. He too was going through a divorce, and we clung to each other like needy children—praising each other and trying to repair the damage done to our torn and shredded egos. I began to feel warm for the first time in months, and the knot in my stomach began to straighten itself out. We had two months together and then it was time for him to go to France for a long-planned sabbatical. He invited me to join him there. He would put me up while I was there if I could get the airfare. It was silly, out of the question. I was unemployed (my husband and I had had a business together, so I was out of a home, a marriage, and a job all at once). But like magic, one day, in the never-ending pile of bills, was a little notice from Continental Airlines, informing me that I was very close to having the mileage to get me a certificate that would take me to Paris. Close but not there.

I called Texas, spoke to a frequent flyer representative, explained the whole situation, said that if she could find a way for me to get the mileage she would be aiding and abetting true love. "That'll be the second time today," she said in her thick Texas accent. It turned out that the little commuter plane that flies from Boston to Cape Cod was a Continental commuter. My parents live on Cape Cod, and I was already planning to go there for Christmas, although I usually took the bus from Boston's Logan Airport to Hanwich. "Make your reservation for Paris now," she told me, "and the minute you take those Cape Cod flights, send me your flight coupons and I'll send you your ticket."

Wow. I was going to Paris. I dined on it, lived on it, dreamed on it.

The flight to my parents was uneventful. But the day of the return trip there was a blizzard. We called the Hyannis airport. No answer. My Dad drove me out there through the terrible snow.

"We're not flying today," the clerk at the desk said, "but why don't you just hop on the bus? Flights are taking off from Boston."

"You don't understand," I said. "If I don't *fly* out of here I don't get to go to Paris." "Ah," the clerk grinned and discussed my plight. "Well, obviously, we'll just have to reschedule you on the next flight out of here."

So I did, I went to Paris. Had a lovely time. Five days in Paris and ten in Toulouse. The high point of the trip was a Thanksgiving dinner that Barry and I gave to honor the professors and their spouses who had been so kind to him. The preparation was a gas—trying to remember the Thanksgiving story as we had learned it in elementary school and translating it into

French. The thrill of a scavenger hunt, looking for Thanksgiving culinary ingredients in Toulouse in February. And the triumph of finding canned cranberries for cranberry sauce. It was a dinner to end all dinners, with everyone speaking each other's languages in varying degrees of skill and ending by singing the folk songs of each country.

I came back to the States. Shortly after Barry returned, he broke up with me, saying that he hadn't meant to get involved in "an exclusive monogamous relationship so soon after his divorce." Six months later he was married. A year and a half later they had a baby.

I will always be grateful to him. He gave me two of the finest weeks of my life, and, I think, was as truthful as he knew how to be, given the utter confusion of being a post-divorce person. I had a lot of healing to do before I could begin to love someone out of wholeness and not emptiness.

The love story is not about Barry. But about the clerk in Texas and the ones in Hyannis. All those strangers who were kind to me during those times: the lawyer who I went to with the final, lingering, hurtful issue, who made me laugh with a story from her own pain and then refused to charge me for our half-hour conversation, the fellow singer in the Minnesota Chorale who treated me to champagne and carrot cake after a performance, the day the divorce was finalized, and the divorce mediator who called to check that I was OK after everything had been agreed upon.

And on and on. When the people we love are kind, there is always an expectation or a hope anyway, that it will be reciprocated. But strangers gain nothing but an increase in the amount of kindness in the universe. I am grateful for that kind of love.

—*Joan Oliver Goldsmith*

PERSPECTIVE

That last story is one of my favorites. Joan Goldsmith has a large and long view of love. She knows that you don't always get what you want, but you can get some deeper understanding of yourself and other human beings while trying to get what you want. She knows that love may not really make the world go around, but you can often get around in the world with love. We are not strangers when it comes to love.

One of the reasons people in my neighborhood eat at a local Sicilian restaurant is because of a sign on its wall: "We reserve the right to serve only those in love, those who have been in love, or those who want to be in love." It's hard to feel alone in the atmosphere created by this sign. And it was easy to get love stories with such clarity of connection declared on the wall. Service has never been refused—the sign is inclusive.

The only thing constant about love is its universality.

The only thing universal about love is its inconstancy.

These truths make coconspirators out of strangers.

I was on my way into the city one Friday evening, more than ready to start my weekend. I had recently broken up with a guy I had dated for a while, so a girl friend and I were ready to go out and meet the men of our dreams, instantly.

I guess you could say I was racing down the highway when I noticed a little black car, with a good-looking male driver, wearing a yellow shirt and keeping a very nice pace with my little red car. He noticed me too and soon we were playing that little car flirting game. You know the one where you pretend to pass so you can get right next to the car and check out the driver. Well, we played this game for a while until one of us, I'm not sure which one, got the courage to wave and smile.

Now of course we've created a bond and we began weaving in and out of traffic together, as if we'd been following each other the whole trip. I felt like I knew this guy and wasn't really thinking too much about the future of this relationship until suddenly he was in the exit only lane. What was he doing?? I wasn't getting off at that exit!! As I approached his car, with a look of panic, the man in the yellow shirt motioned for me to follow him. Well, of course I couldn't do that. A young woman on the freeway following a stranger, however well bonded, off at an exit to who knows where? I don't think so. So, of course I shook my head no and motioned for him to follow me. I guess I figured that if he were a lunatic I'd be safe at my friend's house. I raced ahead and to my surprise he shipped out of the exit lane, almost causing a multiple car accident, and followed me. We remained "together" for a few more miles until we reached my exit. The exit had two sides to it and as I moved to exit, putting my turn signal on with plenty of notice, he exited with me, but took the opposite side of the exit at exactly the time it divided. I watched as he went slowly down the ramp and out of my life as quickly as he had entered it. I was devastated!! I was sure that this was the man God had intended on my marrying. As I got off of the exit I tried to back track and anticipate where he would have gone from his exit, but was unsuccessful in my search.

I arrived at my friend's house disappointed and grief stricken. After explaining the story of my future husband to my friend and getting an hysterical laugh in response, I informed her that the search must not end. I was determined to find the man in the yellow shirt and black car. "OK, OK," she said, "we'll ask every man we see tonight in a yellow shirt what color car he drives."

I'd like to say that the story has a happy ending, that I found my prince charming and that we lived happily ever after, but I never did track him down. I did decide that maybe it was better that I hadn't met my mystery man. Maybe if we had met we would have gone out on a date, gotten into a relationship and ended up with broken hearts. This is the only relationship I've ever had that is filled with ONLY good memories. On another note, I did meet several nice men that night, dressed in yellow, simply by asking them if they'd driven a small black car down I-95 recently. I found that my short love story was actually a very interesting ice breaker and got a chuckle from every person I met that night.

—Lisa Eller,
Toronto, ON,
Canada

I'm an executive for a computer company and I travel a lot to set up training programs for customers. Being alone on the road has its hazards because I'm a single woman and reasonably attractive. When I started traveling a lot, I imagined all kinds of problems, so I took a self-defense course and learned how to maim an aggressive man with my purse and umbrella. I've never had any problems. If anything, my problem is just the reverse. I've never even been politely approached by a man. My problem is that I've become lonely and I'm the one who has started looking around for company.

I often stay in the same hotel in New York, and this past winter there was a most attractive man staying there every time I was. I had a gut-level attraction to him and really wanted to meet him. He made my heart pound. We often passed in the lobby and several times we were in the hotel dining room eating breakfast or dinner alone. The more I saw him, the more I liked what I saw, but I couldn't seem to attract his attention. I began to think of doing stupid things like asking the concierge to find out his name and room number or trying to be in the elevator with him. My mother didn't raise me to be that kind of girl, so I had a love affair with him in my imagination at a distance.

He was there in March. On Thursday morning, we ate breakfast alone in the dining room at separate tables. My heart was pounding again and I kept staring at him, but he just read his newspaper. The next morning, when I was packing to leave, the maid came to me and said she was really worried about something. A man had come to her the day before, carrying a pillow from his bedroom. He had offered her $200 to trade his pillow for one from my room, telling her we were lovers who were having a fight and he just wanted to be able to sleep on my pillow. It would make him happy. When she described the man, I knew it was him. A secret admirer after all.

The maid needed the money and she didn't think it would do any harm, so she gave him my pillow, took his and put a fresh pillowcase on it and put it on my bed. Now she was afraid she might have done something wrong. I said it made me happy to know all this and I would pay her $200 to get me his pillow and keep quiet.

I haven't seen him since. I haven't tried to find out who he is because he must have his own reasons for not approaching me. I slept on his pillow and I admit it smelled really good to me. If he reads this, I wish him dreams as sweet as mine.

—as told to R. F.

In love? Well, maybe.

It was his voice that first tugged at my heart. A clear tenor voice filling the chapel of our church building many years ago. His voice, then his eyes, locked on mine as if a force had drawn us together. He was tall with dark hair that was beginning to thin on top, and brown eyes: dark brown eyes with thick, dark eyebrows that almost met at the bridge of his nose.

We were at his mother's funeral. He had come from another town to sing during the funeral service. I had been asked, along with a number of other ladies in our church, to provide food and serve a luncheon to the family when they returned from the cemetery.

As the first few notes floated across the room, my breath caught in my throat and I seemed to hold that breath while my heartbeat speeded up a notch or two faster than normal. I couldn't stop looking at his eyes. I tried. I looked at the pianist, the casket and the ceiling. But, my eyes kept returning to his, pulled by a force unexplained, unexplainable. What is the force that draws two people together, for a moment, for a lifetime, or for an eternity?

Just as I and the other ladies from the kitchen sat down at an empty table to grab a few bites to eat, "he" walked across the room toward us and moved behind me.

He rested both of his hands on my shoulders, leaned slightly sideways and down so I could turn to see his face. Electric impulses, shock waves, traveled through those warm hands into my shoulders and made me tingle.

He chatted for a few minutes with a few of the women at the table that he obviously knew, and by then I had fallen in love.

I fell in love with that stranger that day. My heart skipped, my skin tingled, and I felt like I was glowing from the top of my head to the tips of my fingers. I wanted to get to know him, spend some time with him, to discover who he was and what he was. Don't get me wrong, I was contentedly married and had three children as well. But who can explain the human reactions sometimes.

I found out his name as the conversation at the table continued, and where he worked through some casual questioning. I even went to his hobby store one day a week or two later, but he wasn't there. Then, I got busy with my husband and three little children and have never seen or even heard about the man since, even though I now live in the same town as he did then.

It was a good feeling at the time—sort of gave me a lift in spirits for a while, and made a pleasant break in the drudgery of being a wife and mother in a busy life. It was a little like watching a fabulous sunset from a hill. It brings a beautiful feeling of peace and serenity that restores the soul and lifts the spirits, then sinks beyond the horizon, only to remain in an almost forgotten memory.

—Wanda Harris,
Idaho Falls, ID

I work in a jewelry store. One day a young woman came into the store and I stepped up to wait on her for I was immediately attracted to her. (Waiting on customers is usually not part of my job duties.) She was perhaps twenty or twenty-one years old, nice figure, brown hair and eyes, and magnetic to me. She had a ring to sell and reluctantly presented it to me for an offer. As I examined it, she related that her husband had been killed and that she just couldn't keep it any more. I got the clear impression from the sound of her voice that by selling her ring she was again saying good-bye, for good.

(I've seen all types and heard all of the "sad" stories, I knew this girl was real.) As she spoke I saw her lip tremble and her eyes begin to shine with tears she refused to let fall. I could not stand there anymore. I became a coward in the face of emotion with a stranger. I asked another employee to finish the purchase as I retreated to my work space and watched her follow through with her decision and walk away.

I felt like I had to touch her, but knew I couldn't. But I had to. I retrieved her name and address information (taken from her driver's license for the purchase order ticket), feeling driven to write to her. I opened the letter by hoping that she would not perceive me too bold to write in such a way. I told her that I admired her courage to do what she did, alone. I told her I felt she would do well in life with her attitude of continuing on. I got quite sentimental in relating to her how I wished my path in life had been different so I could have found someone like her. I concluded with the "do not stand at my grave and weep" poem with the hope of it being of consolation to her.

Without a second thought, I mailed the letter. Days passed imagining what she would think, how she might respond. My emotions ran from remorse and regret to fantasy encounters filled with hope. After about two weeks, the letter came back "addressee unknown." She had moved on with her life, for sure. I was crushed.

—*Anonymous*

It started simply enough. Home on a break from college, I returned to my high school for an "alumni day"—to see friends I had left behind or who had scattered among the great colleges of the country and favorite teachers who, it turned out, were more than a match for most of my college professors.

When I first saw her, she was sitting on an inside window ledge in the lunchroom. She was both apart from and part of a small group of students who were eating and talking. That she could be detached and involved at the same time was intriguing, if only because I often found myself in a similar position. She was wearing jeans and a white shirt and clogs and had short hair. That I had seen her here—at the place which had allowed me to learn so much about myself—was comforting.

Lights did not flash. Electricity did not surge. Doves did not break into flight. Although she was, and is, beautiful, there was no VA-VA or VOOM. Just a calm captivation. And an image that remained consistently sharp and clear of a young woman who for some strange reason left me to believe we shared a soul. I asked someone nearby for her name.

That encounter caused me once again to think about fate and coincidence and how easy it is to confuse the two—if in fact they are different. Always tending toward skepticism, it is still difficult to dismiss as pure happenstance certain events—such as the lingering vision which drew me to see her again.

Nearly ten years after that first encounter—which was an encounter for me only—I decided to do something about that image which did not dim with time of a young woman on a window ledge. We now lived far apart—she still in our home town and I on the opposite side of the country. Home for Christmas, I sought to find her.

From our high school alumni office I learned that she worked as a finance professional for a major national firm in a big office in the city. I called the office, and posing as a potential client, explained that I wanted to meet with "her" to discuss my financial planning needs. Despite rather persistent and irritating attempts by the receptionist to steer me to other professionals in the office, I finally was able to schedule a meeting for the next day.

Money is not generally the first—or even second or third—topic I normally discuss with a new acquaintance, particularly not my money. But I had gotten myself into this one. I needed to "describe in detail my financial situation" so she would "assess my needs properly." She certainly had the big-firm lingo down pat. But she was also quite down-to-earth and charming. I was captivated again.

We stayed in touch from afar for the next year. Then I returned home. Despite my excellent imitation of a jerk from time to time, she did not write me off. She said yes when I asked her to marry me. Whether fate or mere coincidence, I'm happy.

—L. B.

It all started about twelve years ago. A friend of mine was sent to jail for what I can't remember now, well it doesn't matter anyway. He wrote and said, "I have a friend, his name is Bob; would you like to write him too?" I said sure, but I wasn't going to get serious with anyone in jail. So, we wrote to each other for about two years and then I started to make trips up to visit him on visiting days.

Our first visit was terrible. I was scared to death of him. He is twelve years older than I am and has one blue eye and one brown eye. But, he was very nice to me and we hit it off just fine. We really got to be best friends and sort of soul mates, I guess you could say. I love this man very much despite his faults and past life. One day on a visit, he asked me to marry him, and with my strange sense of humor I said, "Sure, when you get out and I have a free Saturday." Not ever thinking it would really happen, but on the other hand very excited and sort of worried all at the same time. Bob is very old fashioned in many ways. He asked my mother and father if they would mind an ex-convict in the family. They accepted him with open arms. I know all of this sounds crazy, but it really happened this way. I can remember it just as if it were yesterday. We have our share of arguments and fights, but we seldom go to sleep at night without saying "I love you" and we usually never go to bed mad. I know it's hard to believe, but it's true.

When Bob came home, we lived with my parents for a while and were married. We have now been married for eleven years and I'll tell you the truth, it has been "for better or for worse" just like the vows say!

I really believe the reason we have made it this far (when our friends and no one else thought we would) is because of God, honesty and the fact that we became best friends first. I mean before emotions or sex or anything else were involved. Isn't that how it's supposed to be? I trust him as much as I trust my mother! I gave him a chance in life and he has given me back so much more. I really love this man with all my heart. So, here is a real love story for you.

—Cynthia Shank,
Milwaukee, WI

PERSPECTIVE

One of the most popular categories of love stories related to me was about going back to look for love in the past. High school and college reunions were the chief hunting grounds. We go to find out how much things are still as they used to be.

The letters received on this subject admitted old love is not always what's looked for—they looked for youth or sex or a wild good time. Love-the-first-time and love-the-first-time-it-really-mattered is usually not the same love. And neither one is waiting at the receiving line at reunions.

One reunion veteran wrote to say that his old girl was still not the love of his life, she was only the great one-night stand she always was, but he wasn't unhappy about finding that out again.

For my own part I decided to find the fifteen-year-old girl I was in love with when I was a nineteen-year-old singing cowboy on a ranch in Colorado. 1956. A summer I would live over in a minute. The problem was that her family was fancy folks from the upper crust of St. Louis and I was trash from Texas. Her father wrote to me—said stay away from my daughter—you're not good enough for her. Though I was outraged at the time, when I look back from age sixty and know what I know now, I can't blame him. I would have told me to stay away from his daughter if I had been in his shoes.

I was afraid to tell him to go to hell—so I told her. She never wrote back. That was forty years ago. But the cowboy still loves the girl from St. Louis. So. With the excuse of doing research for this book, I hired a private detective to find my long-lost love.

The private eye found her in four hours. Cost me $272. Computerized databases have made finding the lost easy. The investigator gave me something to *ponder, though: Does this person want you to find her? And will the reality of what you find be worth giving up the memory?*

I don't know. Not yet. I wrote. She hasn't written back. Yet.

I imagine a nice lady telling her husband she's heard from the Trash from Texas again and won't write him this time either. My wife certainly hopes this is the case. My wife says the Beauty from St. Louie is probably the Bad News Lady from Beaumont by now. I suspect she's right.

The cowboy is polishing his boots and combing his hair just in case. He was a fool for love then—and a fool for love still.

I have been involved with a charming man for some time. He makes me feel radiant and beautiful at the start of every day. He uses luscious terms of endearment, appreciates me completely, and is sensitive to my every mood. He is the Egyptian man from whom I buy my coffee early each morning on the way to the office. He has made serving coffee a passionate and generous encounter. All he wants in exchange is a smile. I'm ready for anything after enjoying that big grin and those warm words. I can't imagine taking on the day without him.

—*Anonymous*

For two years, we were best friends. We were lovers. We laughed together. We cried together. We spent every waking hour that we were away from our jobs together. Both of us had gone through a divorce, so marriage was the last thing on our minds. It was never brought up!

Now, here we were, side-by-side on our knees going through the treasures in my mother's old trunk, since I was executrix of her will.

"Look, here's an envelope addressed to you, Renie!" Bud exclaimed. "There's something bulky in it."

The note read: *To my dear daughter, I give this ring. Your loving mother.* Many things went through my mind, and I remembered seeing this beautiful ring on my mother's finger before she and Dad divorced when I was thirteen.

I put the ring on my finger and commented, "Dad and Mom were married July 3, 1923."

Bud turned to me and said, "Why don't we get married July 3 and use your mother's ring."

"Yeah," I said jokingly, "that would save you a few bucks!" He was so frugal he'd squeeze a penny until it squeaked.

That was thirty years ago, and we'll celebrate our wedding anniversary July 3, 1995.

People always notice my ring as it's very different and still so beautiful. Bud gets a twinkle in his eye as he recounts our story, only it's his version: "We were on our knees, going through her mom's old trunk," he says, "when she found the ring and asked me to marry her."

I've always let him have his fun because, after all, I got my man! He's still my handsome, wonderful buddy. We've been soul mates thirty years.

—Irene Renie Peterson,
Bellingham, WA

Yeah I sure as hell had a torrid love affair in my mind and on paper for many months with a fellow aspiring poet at the club where we used to meet and pour our hearts out each week. God knows I wrote dozens of poems about him—the most stunning looking young man of about thirty-five. With myself going on fifty-odd years, my heart used to be in my mouth and that too was dry enough—short of breath, dizzy in the head, just couldn't think straight—imagine a broad my age acting like a teenager—God I enjoyed that agony steamy, sensuous and stunning.

Well, that went on for quite some time, my what a dither I was in, all I could do was look at him, look deeply into his beautiful black eyes. Being vain and aware of his looks and his effect on me, he played the game back with his black curls flopping just at the right angle of his face to heighten his smile. We made love with our eyes and poured our hearts out in poetry, he verbally and me in the written word. I was too petrified to read aloud—there was so much passion. I just smoldered.

At least we were together as lovers on paper and so that was how I endured my great love and illusion.

God the inspiration that came from those emotions was unbelievable. I laugh about it and it was quite a positive experience.

P.S. By the way, I only read my love poems the weeks he wasn't there and many of my friends were curious to know who he was and who could turn a reasonably sane and somewhat odd woman on her head, ah, but how I loved every moment of that torment and think of those days with a great deal of nostalgia and a big grin on my face as I write these words.

—M. S.,
St. James,
West Australia

I am heartily in favor of high school reunions.

"Why would you be?" some of my friends ask. "You just sit around and talk about your aches and pains. You live in the past. You remember better what happened fifty years ago than what happened this morning!"

Not so. At least, not to the extent some people may think. Yes, we're older. We do brag about our grandchildren a lot and our memories are mainly sweet. But we're forward-looking, too.

Consider my case. The N. S. High School class to which I belonged graduated in 1935. However, I didn't graduate with them. My family had moved from Smalltown to Salt Lake City in 1933 and I graduated from South High School.

However, I had an occasional contact with the Smalltown crowd. When they started to hold reunions, they made contact with me and sometimes I made it. In about 1981, I came to a reunion from my home in Southern California where I had retired after having lived there for twenty years.

I recognized most of the people. . . . some didn't recognize me. But one person I recognized immediately because the ravages of years had not changed her that much. She was Maurine. We immediately fell to comparing notes about the intervening years and found that we were both alone.

Two months later, I asked her for a dinner date. We hit it off well and I began coming about every month to see her. It was readily apparent to me, after a year or so, that I was in love with her. She was not so sure. However, I pressed my case and she eventually consented to marry me.

So, we were married in February 1983 . . . fifty years after we had last gone to school together. Since then, we have traveled extensively, found we are very compatible, and in a few days will attend another high school reunion . . . sixty years from graduation.

Don't remind me of the aches and pains of aging or the loss of memory. I am having too much fun just living the present with a companion who understands my foibles and weaknesses. My children and grandchildren love her, too. No wonder I am in favor of high school reunions.

—*W. O.*

Last October, 1990, my cousin and I went on what we considered to be "the vacation from God"—a seven-day cruise to the Caribbean. I had lost seventeen pounds for this grand excursion and was looking great—my intentions, to have a meaningless, commitment-free seven-day frolicking fling with some Caribbean stud.

I met a pale English type looking guy with blond hair and blue eyes. He was the answer to my prayers. This guy, I decided, I should try to make my constant companion. The next day we arrived in Grand Cayman Islands. This guy was sooooo much fun. The freest spirit I had ever met. So full of life—everything you could ever wish to be. He had a love and appreciation for everything in life and was always one hundred percent positive. I fell, head over heels! We spent the next three days together. He never even once kissed me. It was so exciting and romantic.

The next three months we wrote (daily) and called (daily) and I had never been so happy in my life. The anticipation of a letter, the excitement of making a phone call. All of the love poured into baking cookies and sending care packages. I was in love with love and romance. December 1990, I packed my California bags and flew to Pennsylvania for a long weekend. Everywhere I went, I had roses. A fireplace table at dinner. A surprise party in my honor, a billboard welcome, a radio dedication of his love and a home cooked meal from his mom. How could I say no to a marriage proposal on New Year's 1991.

January 1991, five days short of my packing up my life in Southern California and moving to the snow, he came out to visit. Suddenly, the wind changed directions—my feet were so cold they held their ground in Southern California. I had quit my job, sold my car, had my twenty-four years of life in boxes, shaken up my family and friends. . . . He had remodeled his home, bought a "family" type car and was searching for a promising job with mucho $ for our new unchained life together. The freest spirit I ever knew, the happiest man in Pennsylvania, the one who appreciated life to the fullest and . . . loved me . . . or the idea of me as I loved the idea of him.

What I realized was that I was more in love with the idea than the man, and explaining it to him was the hardest thing ever.

But I have never been happier or felt so romantic or loved love so much as I did in those five months. For that I am so grateful and I will never forget him. Love is truly a wondrous thing.

—Cathy Cavallo,
San Bernadino, CA

The most endearing love story I know is the story of my cousin Ann Foster. All of her lifetime, she remained single as Miss Ann Getz of Morton, Illinois. Then after fifty-six years of separation, her high school sweetheart, Jack Foster, re-entered her life. Over the years he had married and raised a family. Now his wife had died and he contacted the wonderful young woman to whom he had written poetry at Morton High School. Remembering him fondly, she had kept those poems all this time. They exchanged many phone calls and letters and soon decided to get married. And so, Miss Ann Getz became Ann Foster at age 80. She was a lovely bride. Ann and Jack shared two intensely happy years together before he died suddenly during surgery. Ann had won such a place in Jack's family circle that his children and their families still keep in contact with her, visiting her and inviting her to their homes for holidays.

—Lissa Thompson,
West Bountiful, UT

She was a beautiful Pom Pom team member/cheerleader for the university we both attended and I was a spectator of both the basketball games and of her wonderful dancing. She was so lovely that my father even made mention of the fact that he would adopt her if ever given the chance. I would jokingly ask my father, when I would leave my seat, "... to keep an eye on my girlfriend." This was an innocent bit of fun for the two of us. We enjoyed the thought of knowing the "lovely little brown girl with the cute legs." Although I was constantly encouraged by my father and his friends, I never introduced myself to her. I suppose I did not want to ruin the thought of her being "my girlfriend."

The following year I graduated from the university and moved to a large city and began my career. One of my best friends was getting married and I was asked to be an attendant and usher at this wedding. As the crowd began to gather, I noticed a young lady enter the church. I immediately called "dibs" to the rest of the guys. "Fellas, stay back, I get to seat the lady in the green dress!" As I walked her to her seat, I realized I would like to talk to this lady for a long time. Although we were not able to talk much that night, we did exchange telephone numbers.

During our first date we discussed many topics and seemed to have much in common. Surprisingly, one of the things we have in common is our alma mater. We both inquired into each other's activities at school and involvement in campus organizations. Her answer was that she was on the nationally recognized Stephen F. Austin State University Pom Pom Squad. My heart began to pound and my hands began to sweat and my mouth became very dry. "You were the girl on the end with the uh, uh really nice tan!" Yes, that was her, sitting across from me smiling!

This story is a gift from God. Well, it is and she is. Her name is Navaz, from an ancient Persian language, and it means "Gift from God."

God has answered my prayers of meeting the one He has chosen for me. We were married on December 18, 1993, and are very thankful for the two friends that were married and allowed us to actually meet each other, this time, in person.

—Jeff Dickerson,
Houston, TX

I had left my hometown, San Francisco, to study cello for a year at the Royal College of Music in London. During that time, I had lived with a titled family and had acquired a very broad English accent. Now I was on my way back to San Francisco, via New York City, where I had planned to stay over for a week. I looked up my very first cello teacher who, when I phoned him, said, "Come right over to my studio, we are having a quartet rehearsal—I want to hear about your experiences in London, and I think you will enjoy hearing my quartet." I found his studio, and listened to a great performance of a Beethoven quartet, and then was introduced to my teacher's colleagues. One of them, the violist, had been giving the other musicians instructions about how he thought the music should be played. I thought he was the most conceited man I had ever met—or so he seemed, after the laid-back English members of "my" London home. Well, we began to date and I realized he was not conceited—just very sure of himself. One night, he invited me to have dinner and go to the theater. I met him near Carnegie Hall, wearing a long formal gown (we had dressed for dinner every night in London) and he took me down 57th Street to the Automat, and then to a movie! He hardly spoke to me (he claims my English accent inhibited him), but he had a lot of jokes to relate. Now we began to date almost every night. I canceled my ticket home, just in case. We took many trips on the Staten Island ferry and sometimes we parked at the Palisades in New Jersey, overlooking Manhattan's fabulous skyline. He didn't even hold my hand. Finally, I thought this was ridiculous, and one night, I said, "I think we should get married." His answer? "O.K., when?" Not taking any chances, and having grown more and more fond of this guy (I had always wanted to marry a musician), I said, "Tomorrow." We got a license and eloped to Greenwich, Connecticut, where I had the weird idea that divorce would be easier than in New York.

It's now many years and two wonderful young ones later. We never had time to divorce and I'm so happy that I had the nerve to propose!

P.S. He's still telling jokes!

—V. K., Seattle, WA

PERSPECTIVE

A wisecracking friend read these stories and said, "There's no sex in here. Why no sex? How can you have love stories without sex? The closest people came was saying they got 'tingly'—especially in letters from Utah—there's a lot of 'tingly' out there in Utah—why?"

The easy answer is that nobody wrote to me about sex—at least not the graphically explicit kind. One man told me about loving a Jersey cow when he and she were both young, but despite what you might assume, he insisted the love was strictly platonic. He never even kissed her.

A better answer is that my friend needs to read more closely—he missed all the sex somehow. Almost all the stories have a clear dimension of sexuality in them. Sensuality is woven into the stories. Touch and smell. Lust. Erotic imagination. Kisses and hugs. And the inexpressible feelings that are pointed at by OHWOW *and* WHOOHAA *and* OHMYGOD*—the "tingling," the pounding heart and dizzy head. Ecstasy. Couples spend undescribed miracle weekends together, get pregnant and have children. There are allusions to private fantasies that lead to pleasure as well as trouble. There's plenty of sex in these stories—you just have to read between the lines.*

We did get some wild stories about men falling in love with women they've seen in triple-X movies and magazines. And we got some interesting stories from women who spoke of erotic friendships being as good as love affairs, as if making love and having sex are really the same thing. I wonder. Love usually takes years and the sex usually takes minutes. To be faithful in body but not in mind, or to be faithful in mind but not in body—these are dangerous styles of love. Still, we got the letters and I'll stand by the statement that true love is whatever people say it is.

As for "tingly"—I've felt "tingly" a few times myself. You don't have to live in Utah. If you look at the statistics on birthrates in Utah, however, you could conclude a lot of "tingly" does occur there and has the usual consequences.

When I first saw him, my heart smiled. An acquaintance of my husband's. A lower-on-the-totem-pole G.I. that my husband befriended while stationed at a far-from-home military base.

The next time I saw him was three years later. He was passing through town and he stopped by to say "hello." Once again, my heart smiled but this time it also giggled.

Thirteen years passed. Then I found that we were moving to his hometown. My heart laughed, for it knew things I chose not to know, let alone remember.

Finally, we were there: his wife, my husband, me and, of course, him. My husband insisted that he be my card partner as they all attempted to teach me a card game. So, every Friday evening for months, we made love, right there in his kitchen—as we all played cards.

Well, time and life march on. My husband's job would be taking us to a different town. I bid him farewell—and in a moment I shall always hold dear—he kissed me. Not on the cheek or forehead—but, lips to lips—and he held me in an embrace I won't soon forget. And his eyes saw my heart and mine his and they pounded in silent unison.

It was wonderful! His kiss was freedom for my dreams.

We now live a thousand miles apart. He knows. I know. And our hearts smile.

—Linda D. Fallon,
Waynesburg, PA

I had returned home, a tiny, nondescript town in the northeast corner of Oklahoma, to celebrate the holidays with my extended family. It was Christmas 1985, and I was alone, single still, divorced for so long that I had trouble remembering how bad the experience of marriage had been for me.

In fact, I had grown accustomed to life alone by then, after eighteen years of living on my own in the midst of bustling Los Angeles, struggling to make ends meet as a dental assistant, single-handedly raising a daughter, dating as the rare opportunity arose.

I was waiting for Mr. Right, I suppose, although the truth is, I had pretty much given up on him. Or anyone who even bore a faint resemblance to him. It wasn't as if LA didn't offer some interesting, very eligible men. Nor had I lost my knack for attracting such a one on occasion. Never the *right* one, however. It was looking more and more as though the man of my dreams was just that—a dream.

I had, over the years, become a city girl and expected to remain that way permanently, though I still looked forward to those visits back to my roots in Oklahoma every few years or so, renewing family ties, breathing fresh air. It was especially good doing some of the old things we had always done together as a family, for instance, everybody dressing up and heading for church on Sunday morning, that little country church of native stone and stained glass—where so much of my childhood had been spent, where my values had been instilled and my faith shaped. It always felt right being there. It was a place where I belonged. So, come Christmas 1985, there we were, lined up in our family pew.

At promptly 10 a.m., the Reverend Marshall took his seat in the high-backed chair next to the altar and looked out on his congregation. Straight into my soul! Our eyes became locked onto one another for a brief, unsettling moment. My heart seemed to literally leap inside me.

It scared me to feel what I felt just then. I had not been prepared for this in any sort of way. I had not laid eyes on this man before, a stranger to the community, as far as I was concerned, though he had been at the church for a few years by that time. I had heard about him, briefly, the fact he was unattached, that's all, and well received by the congregation.

But this! A preacher, for goodness sake.

It couldn't be. These were the persons I had been raised to respect, to revere, to hold sacred, certainly never to fall in love with. He may be eligible, even somewhat attractive, but he was still a man of the cloth. In other words, a bit more godly than human. Which meant this whole thing presently swimming around in my head was simply unthinkable. I avoided his eyes the rest of the hour, as well as any thoughts or feelings of the kind. I tried my best to remain numb.

On the way out of the church, I hid, like some silly school girl. I hid behind my sister, so I wouldn't have to face the preacher or, worse, exchange a handshake and conversation, to have to meet his eyes. I figured on disappearing into the flow of traffic, passing inconspicuously out the front door and back to California. I took considerable pride in my ability to stay out of trouble, to avoid messy problems.

I made it as far as the car, actually. That's when the big front doors of the church flew open and the Reverend Marshall announced from the top of the steps that pizza was on him that day. Everyone, he said, was invited.

It was *me* he was inviting, of course. His feelings seemed to be as crazy and as obvious as mine, though we were trying our best to disguise them. We both knew something special was in the making that crisp December afternoon, something much more than pepperoni.

That became apparent from the first bite, sharing pizza with the pastor and his flock, turning Pizza Hut into another worship service. We did, after all, take up an offering—to help defray the expenses. The pastor's contribution remained, nonetheless, in the generous triple digits. Money, though, well spent, he is now quick to point out. And who am I to disagree with the Reverend Mr. Right, love at first bite.

We were married that following Easter Sunday, in that little country church where I had come to know my Maker, as well as the man my dreams had been made of.

—Gretchen Marshall,
San Antonio, TX

Everyone called him J.C. He was tall, slender, strong, had a wonderful handlebar mustache and a twinkle in his eye. He was a true adventurer. He loved to climb to the top of mountains . . . or explore caves inside the earth. To look at the stars, and study physics (working on a Ph.D.). To play music (stand-up bass) and dance. . . . To ride a horse or his Harley . . . but most all, he loved to fly.

I met him in a small rural town where I had moved for a year to take a break from "city life" and study photography. I never actually spent time with him alone . . . but there was always something there. I don't know what to call it. He was the kind of person who made everything feel better just by his presence . . . and I immediately saw and felt that . . . and somehow I think he felt that way about me. Our exchange was one of smiles, recognition, warmth and appreciation—all done with a look. Words really weren't necessary. We SAW each other . . . that simple, genuine acknowledgment from the heart that the other is there.

I was surprised when I moved away (to another state) that J.C. stayed in contact with me. He would randomly write or call and occasionally visit when he happened to be passing through the city. It was during these next eight years that our friendship grew to a true love.

I don't know why, but for some reason, it never seemed to be a romantic, sexual exchange. Not that it couldn't have been . . . just that what our exchange was really about was so much more than that. He remarried and I both knew and liked his wife. Our friendship stayed true. For whenever we did see each other, we were able to share all the real and deep stuff going on inside . . . and we somehow were able to be encouraging and comforting and supportive of each other—and we didn't even particularly *do* anything to make it that way. We simply were there for each other . . . and knew it. What a special thing. To really love someone and not need to have anything from it . . . to just be able to feel it and cherish it for what it is. I was lucky to have J.C. in my life. He is the only person (and probably will remain so) that periodically called my answering machine for no other reason than to leave the message "I love you."

The last time I saw him, he was moving to the Southwest. We ran into each other back in the small town where we'd originally met. As often as we talked about doing so, we had never gone flying together. He looked at his watch and said, "Well, we've got about an hour and a half of daylight left—let's go." So up we went, in his two-seater Cessna with the sun spreading golden orange over the Cascade mountains. It was beautiful. And J.C. glowed with his love for flying that plane. As we left the hangar, he turned to me and said: "I don't want this to weird you out . . . but I just want you to know that if anything happens to me and I die in a plane crash . . . it will be okay . . . because I love this soooooo much." And, yes, I *did* know what he meant.

Five months later, I got a phone call. J.C. died in a plane crash in New Mexico. I cried and cried myself to sleep that night. But, you know, just before I went to sleep, clear as a bell, I heard him . . . and he was laughing. He said, "Well, guess I fell into a black hole. . . ." And even though I miss him so, I know it *is* okay. I see him soaring high and free. And I believe he too can hear me saying, "I love you."

—B. J.

PERSPECTIVE

Love can be connected to an object. It's why we have drawers and boxes and trunks full of keepsakes whose meaning is known only to us. And sometimes love lies casually about us—attached to the most common things.

In a drawer in the kitchen of our houseboat is an incomplete set of tableware—for everyday use. Stainless steel knives and forks and spoons with teak handles. Dansk design. I've been using these implements for almost forty years. These were the first things my first wife and I selected as wedding presents. We got the whole set. Several place settings are missing now because my children used them in the sandpile in the backyard when they were small. Some of the teak handles have teeth marks in them, left by Findley, the beagle—a dog who could not be cured of chewing things. He was sent away to live with a lady who would put up with him.

When I left the house of the first marriage, one of the few things I wanted was this set of tableware. It connected me to daily life with my children. As I have moved from house to house, the knives and forks and spoons have moved with me, maintaining some continuity with my past. My oldest son would like to have these utensils when I die—to pass on to his son.

I admire these knives and forks and spoons. Useful, lasting, and still elegant to look at and hold. This cannot be said of many things I have. Not even of me.

Holding a scratched and teeth-marked spoon while eating my Cheerios this morning, I reflected on its connections with love. I once loved the woman who helped me select it. I loved the houses it has been in. My children and I loved the dog who loved chewing the spoon. I love the memories of the mornings spent using the spoon in all the seasons of the years of my life. I love *the woman who sits across from me now as these thoughts come to mind. I love the son who loves the spoon still—and love the grandson who will sit and eat his Cheerios with it someday. I hope he loves his life as much as I have loved mine. If only the spoon could talk, it would tell him a great deal.*

Especially about the love that connects all these people, present and past, large and small. Love is embedded in all of this practical, sentimental, confusing stuff—visible in the scrapbooks of memory—and if you look carefully, just visible in the curved simplicity of an old spoon sitting in an empty bowl at breakfast.

Amtrak—Richmond, VA, to D.C. I was exhausted. I had been up til 3 a.m. the night before and then back up at seven. Glad to find the train mostly empty. Sat on the right-hand side—spreading myself and my stuff on both seats. Just before the train left, a man sat down in the two vacant seats across the aisle from me. We smiled briefly. Pleasant enough. And then we proceeded to occupy ourselves privately in our own worlds. He was absorbed in some paper shuffling and repacking his leather case with computer, etc. I was emptying film from my camera and organizing my camera gear. Mission accomplished, I was ready for my much needed afternoon nap. I repositioned myself turning sideways, curling up my legs and resting my head on its left side against a now partially reclined seat. It was then that I actually looked at this man across from me. He was looking straight ahead . . . lost in his own thoughts. I closed my eyes and instantly the image of his shoulder was there. So, in my dreams, I put my head on his shoulder and fell asleep—oh, so peacefully.

Perhaps an hour or more passed. When I opened my eyes, he was asleep in the exact position of my mind's eye. I thought I was still dreaming. But, then he moved. And his eyes opened. And he looked at me. Our eyes locked. I could not look away. I could not talk. I can only describe it as an incredibly intimate moment. I could not move and yet everything was immensely alive. It was like falling into an infinite universe and yet being an intricate part of the whole thing. It transcended time but I know this continued for longer than was normally comfortable, even with someone you already knew. Finally, it became too intense—as the conscious mind clicked in—wanting an explanation. We both looked away at the same time. I had no idea what had happened. I stared out the window at the passing landscape with a blank mind and a full heart. Arlington, VA, next stop. The train slows down. I am a bit afraid to look in his direction again, but eventually I do. He is staring down at his hands. His right index finger is touching the wedding band on his left. I don't know what happened next. I closed my eyes. And put my head back on his shoulder and went to sleep.

—Natasha M.,
San Francisco, CA

My head exploded in a blaze of crimson. Tiny pinpoints of light flashed on and off, dancing before my eyes.

Voices above me. "Is she badly hurt? Should we go for an ambulance?"

I was on the ground. Someone was holding my head in his lap. I tried to sit up but the world tilted and dropped me off the edge. Swimming back to consciousness, Ernie's face came into focus, worried and scared.

"Bonnie—are you all right? How do you feel?"

I tried to speak, but my mouth wouldn't cooperate.

"What—what happened?"

"One of the race cars threw a big clod of dirt and grass up from the tires and it hit you in the head." Ernie eased me into a sitting position until my head rested on his shoulder. I had thought I might wind up in Ernie's arms that day, but this was ridiculous!

For once, I was embarrassed to be the center of attention. People slowly started drifting away when they saw I wasn't badly hurt. My mouth must have been open when I got hit, because I kept spitting dirt, a very unromantic thing to do when you're out on a first date with someone you want to impress.

There was dirt in my mouth, dirt up my nose, in my eyes, and in my ear. I was a bleary-eyed, runny-nosed, dirt-drooling young woman who wished she could crawl under the nearest bush and hide.

Actually, Ernie was the third guy to ask me for a date that Fourth of July in 1950.

Elmer had asked me first. He was a good buddy, more like a brother than a boyfriend. I was comfortable with him. He always reminded me of a big, good-natured bear. Tall, with an early beer paunch, he wore Coke bottle glasses and got along with everyone. My second invitation came from Jerry. Now, Jerry was MY kind of man! VERY tall, black curly hair, and brown eyes you could drown in. He had shoulders a yard wide, no hips, and looked like he could bite chains in half. He was a member of the local motorcycle club, wore his jeans tight, and could whinny like a stallion so realistically he could make a mare nervous.

So why did I turn down one comfortable old shoe date and another with Mr. Fantastic for a date with Ernie?

He was certainly nothing to write home about. Skinny to the point of emaciation, his chest curved in, instead of out. He was tall, a six foot hoe handle of a man. His clothes clung desperately to him, trying to find a place to hang on. I think what got to me was the slightly bewildered look on his face. He positively oozed the need to be mothered.

He had been coming into the restaurant where I worked as a waitress, draping himself on an end stool, and dawdling over his supper much longer than necessary. He always seemed so lonesome, so lost. He began shyly striking up a conversation whenever possible, and finally, nervously asked, "Would you care to go out with me on the Fourth of July?"

"Well, maybe," I answered, "I'll let you know in a couple of days." Wouldn't do to let on that he interested me very much.

So here I was, sitting in a cow pasture near Sedro Wooley, where Ernie and I had gone from the Loggerodeo to watch a bunch of clunky cars race around a field, throwing up cow pies and chunks of turf, like the one that had clobbered me in the head.

He helped me get shakily to my feet, and we slowly made our way to his car. He lowered me into the seat, then loped away and soon returned with two icy Cokes.

"Do you want to go home?" he asked, rubbing my shoulder, his blue eyes troubled.

"Well, maybe just to clean up and change," I said, looking down at my formerly white blouse and pants, now streaked and splattered with dirt, drool and for all I knew cowpies.

Ernie drove me home. I showered and changed into my favorite dress with the gold glitter on the front. My face was now all splotchy red and swollen on one side. As I joined Ernie in the living room he asked, "Do you think a good steak would help?"

"On my eye or internally?" I answered.

We drove to Ted's 99 Cafe. The steaks were sizzling hot, tender, and juicy rare. The rest of the meal was perfect, too, and Patti Page was singing "Tennessee Waltz" on the jukebox.

Ernie sang along for a few bars, and I realized this man couldn't carry a tune in a bushel basket. We spent a long time over our meal, talking, danced a little to the jukebox, and drove back to Bellingham as the moon was rising.

We parked by the lake and watched as colorful displays of fireworks rivaled the brilliance of the moon on the water.

He turned to me and pulled me close. His breath was sweet and clean and he had an exciting man smell about him. His eyes glittered in the moonlight.

"Oh, Bonnie, I like you so much!" he breathed, pulling me tighter and kissing me fervently.

"Ouch," I whispered.

—Bonnie Jean Foster,
Bellingham, WA

Tammy and I met at work. We did lunches and coffee breaks for about a week before our first conversation took place outside of that "controlled environment."

At that time, Tammy was in recovery for addiction. She had that quality of charisma reserved for those who have walked through hell. Our conversation in her apartment that night was intimate; high-charged emotions crackled through our voices as Tammy shared her life experiences. It's neither surprising nor particularly shameful that those high-charged emotions became high-charged hormones. The hugs hung on as I tried to kiss away that broken angel's tears. The kisses hung on. The hugging became petting. The pulse rates went up, the walls came down and—she said "no." I should have typed that in boldface. I should have called CNN. And not just because of the rejection factor.

Because staying clean from drugs, I learned later, was only one aspect of Tammy's problem. Like most addicts, she was cross-addicted. And sex was a heavy weight on that cross.

Tammy surprised herself by saying "no" that night. It was still a new word in her vocabulary, and it had never been tested under these circumstances. But what really blew her away was my request that we remain friends. And we did. That night showed us that men and women could relate intimately without sex.

This opened a new avenue of relating for her. In a small but significant way, this aided her recovery. And, with that, she asked me a question that night that I have learned to ask myself every morning—"How many people have you told you love today?"

And I responded with the only honest answer I could: "Not nearly enough."

Four years later, I still ask myself that question. The funny thing is, I have yet to find a better answer.

I leaned more about love that night than any "girlfriend" has taught me since. It was then that I recognized love as an art, not a scoreboard. Tammy asked the question. The answers are everywhere, in everyone. From all different degrees and perspectives.

Like I said, that was four years ago. Tammy and I are still friends. She is happily married. Her recovery continues. And I continue to make new friends. I'm presently involved with a lady whose own life experiences echo those of Tammy's. We have achieved something almost unheard of in my circle of acquaintances. We are best friends.

—Dean Romanchuk,
Bethlehem, PA

Many families have evolved traditions to help deal with the death of loved ones. In our family we leave symbolic items with them. We have had four significant deaths in my family since 1980. Upholding this family tradition, the following describes my struggle to come up with an item to leave with a very special person.

Many thoughts were racing through my head during the difficult days following the sudden death of my Dad. In February 1989. I felt uncomfortable and ashamed that I had not yet figured out a personal item to leave with Dad. What would be meaningful to Dad and to me?

Dad and I spent countless hours running, skiing, and playing cribbage together. I couldn't leave a cribbage board: it just didn't seem right—nor a ski: impossible due to size. I would, according to my brother, be copying him if I gave Dad a running shoe. At that time the last problem I needed was sibling controversy. Most importantly, I didn't think that would be meaningful enough to me . . .

"I've got it!" I thought, with a great deal of enthusiasm, considering the circumstances. I can draw him a picture. Dad would like that! Realizing that quality would not be an issue, I took out a piece of drawing paper and my pen set. I started by drawing a heart, divided in the middle by a crooked white line. Crooked, I do not know why, but the idea was the separation or loss of love or loves. I would cut the picture in half and give half to Dad and keep the other.

Around the heart I drew racing numbers, running shoes, skis, and a cribbage board. The racing numbers, our consecutive numbers in two races, divided by the line, were from just two of the races we had run together. I put my two numbers on the piece I kept and his two numbers appear on the piece that I put in his casket. Each side of the heart had one of my running shoes next to one of Dad's. I drew our skis—one of each pair, side by side at the top of the heart. The well-used cribbage board was drawn with half of it on each piece.

My Dad, who was also a teacher, coach, and drug educator at my high school, not only spent the majority of his free time with my brother and me, he also taught us to think positively. As a child I was never allowed to say "can't." He would always correct me by telling me to say "I am having trouble." When wishing me success before a sports event, Dad would say "good skill," not "good luck." He taught me that I have control over what I accomplish in life. He instilled in me Henry Ford's philosophy: "Whether you think you can or you think you can't, you are right."

Drawing this broken heart brought me the greatest feeling I had since his death. I took one piece up to the funeral home and set it in the casket, under Dad's hand. I still have the other half, stored in a safe place in my file cabinet.

Although this creation is not the quality seen in an art gallery, it will always remain the most prominent piece in the art gallery of my heart.

—Aaron Burby,
Vashon Island, WA

I am not in the business of writing love stories. Especially not schmaltzy love stories. But I wrote this one because I wanted to debunk some myths. Because I wanted Middle America to know that love is not the sole domain of heterosexuals. And because it's important to me that "the love that dares not speak its name" not only be heard, it be applauded.

After graduating from college, I went alone to South America to travel and work. Three months into my trip I met and fell in love with a Chilean named Carlos. We had a brief but exhilarating love affair. I returned to Berkeley ready to do the traditional thing—find a nice Jewish boy, have a big wedding, make my mother happy.

And then I fell in love. I fell in love hard, crazily, head over heels, unable to do anything but think about how in love I was. We spent two glorious weeks lying in bed, talking and talking, connecting with our minds and our bodies. The only problem was that my new love was a woman. When we met, Jill had been casually dating a man and like me had sworn off women. My mind said, "Katie, this is not a nice Jewish boy. Why make life hard for yourself?" But my heart said, "Katie, you'd be an absolute fool to let this one go."

Well, I listened to my heart. And, thanks to my heart, seven years later I've never been happier. Jill is my best friend and my lover. She is my coconspirator, my confidante and the most unselfconscious person I know. She taught me what it's like to grow up working class. I taught her how to win at Scrabble. Collectively we've been through eight years of medical school, three years of residency, deaths in the family, times of extreme bliss and times of just trying to survive. Our relationship is ever evolving. And in one month our first child will be born.

It's not always been easy. We've had the windshield of our car painted with "We kill homosexuals and we'll get you too." I've struggled against my own homophobia. But it's a struggle I've never regretted. In choosing Jill over waiting for that "nice Jewish boy" I chose love over safety and societal acceptance. And it's the best choice I've ever made.

—Katie Gerstle,
Northampton, MA

While attending college, I happened to be handing out fliers at a meeting and I handed a paper to a young man passing by. He was moving quickly so I didn't get a good look at him, but as I glanced up my body started to tingle from head to toe! (No, not that kind of tingle, the tingle that comes from deep within, like a premonition.) I knew somehow I had to meet this man.

It turned out we had a mutual friend so I begged to be lined up on a date with Mike.

However, the next time I saw him was when he arrived to pick up my roommate for a date. I answered the door (here comes that tingle again), and spent the next 15 minutes talking with him until she was ready to go. We hit it off right from the start.

Needless to say, my roommate only had one date with Mike. Two weeks later, after the quarter ended, Mike called me at my parents' home. We went to a summer cabin with friends for the weekend . . . three days of heaven.

Mike and I never dated another person after that. Three years later we were married. Fourteen years and five children later, we still have date night, every Friday (here comes that tingle again. No, not that kind of tingle, the tingle that says, "I Love You, still").

—Kerrie Kilgore,
Salt Lake City, UT

I remember her vividly, although I would be hard-pressed to describe her appearance in words, other than that she was beautiful. We were at Harvard and acting in a college production of *Guys and Dolls*. She was from a small town in Vermont—the type of place and life that I also loved, which only added to her allure. The rumor was that the director and several others in the show were attracted and had made passes at her, all with no luck: she had a boyfriend up in Vermont, and we were all left to imagine, in envy, this tall, handsome stranger who could hold her love in the face of such temptations.

As the rehearsals went on, she and I became friends, mostly in character. I was Big Jule, the

Chicago gangster, and she was one of the "hot-box" girls in the chorus, to whom an ideal tough-guy like Big Jule was naturally courteous. And so it went. I started escorting her back to her dorm late at night after rehearsal, both of us still partially in character (often still in makeup and costume). She would sometimes invite me in, to continue the conversation, and I would eventually leave—with no more than a peck on the cheek given or sought. Big Jule wouldn't mess with some other guy's doll.

Yet the old-fashioned roles of protector and protected gave a great warmth and security, and our show characters gave our real characters just enough protection from the fears of intimacy to allow for real comfort and connection. We would talk for hours about everything, big and small. Big Jule was head over heels for her, but would do nothing about it. Slowly, through the hours of spoken intimacy, I realized that I was in love with her too, but the decision—and the courage—to break through the roles and express it was even slower in coming. It came on the day of the first performance. After several weeks of rehearsing the role of Big Jule on (and off) stage, I decided that on the walk home after the first show (I think there were four), I would let reality rear its dangerous head, mysterious boyfriend or not.

But the mysterious boyfriend *appeared* at the first show, and the solution to the mystery broke my heart. She had talked about him to me, but never mentioned a last name. Through an extraordinary chain of circumstances, he turned out to be the older brother of a close childhood friend of mine. Big Jule would not mess with another guy's doll. The real me would have, but not when the other guy was the brother of a friend. All characters have their codes to live by.

In hindsight, it probably was for the better. She had remained true to him through other temptations, and there was little reason for me to think that my advances would have met with any more success. More important, whatever direction it took, it would have spoiled the wonderful memory of two characters from a different time and place escorting each other home, so that two real people could talk to each other with an intimacy they might never otherwise have shared.

The show ended. The characters and the excuse to provide an escort evaporated. We bumped into each other a few more times, but the special moments we had shared were over, and their special memory enough to keep. I heard years later that she and the boyfriend were married, and was glad. Every so often, I take the memory out of the fridge, and savor it—as one does a favorite treat at off hours.

—Dan Small,
Boston, MA

I saw him in a nursing home—what we Southerners continue to refer to as an "old folks' home." It's said with respect, not derision.

He was visiting an old man, shooting the breeze. He had all of the necessary characteristics for catching my eye: big, strong, masculine hands; a square jaw; bangs that wouldn't quite stay out of his eyes. I confess that I stared at him a few moments longer than decorum normally allows. He was laughing with the old man, patting him on the back. I was captivated.

Let the other girls daydream about football heroes and the Calvin Klein underwear guy. Give me a man who is good to old folks, patient with little kids, solicitous of stray dogs—it melts my heart every time. He was being kind to the old guy—and he was having fun. For those 45 seconds, I wanted him desperately. I wanted to hold his hand in a dark movie theater. I wanted to invite him to my house for dinner and feed him fried chicken. I wanted to lend him my favorite book. I wanted to walk through the museum with him, arm in arm.

I made my own visit at the nursing home and left without ever having spoken to him.

—Vickie Masters,
Greenville, SC

PERSPECTIVE

Platitudes are poison. Pick up a book of quotations and turn to the love section and you will soon be turned off. The wisdom looks good, but it doesn't look lived in. As this book was assembled I made a list of the really good short lines as they turned up. The list grew to more than a hundred statements. The list was then passed around for readers to consider, with this instruction: "Cut what's clever and cute but not true—cut what you don't believe—cut what you haven't experienced as real." Here's the consensus list of the best sentences from the True Love *stories:*

The opposite of love is not hate, it's indifference.

The game of love is never called on account of darkness or rain.

Most of us need love the most when we're the most unlovable.

Every love story has an unhappy ending, sooner or later.

If you concentrate on giving love, your task will seem small but the results large; if you concentrate on getting love, your task will seem large and the results small.

The basic question of love: If you love me still, will you love me moving?

Some say God is love; some say love is God; I say love is holy.

On the last day that my portable "love stories booth" was in operation, an old black Ford pickup parked at the curb. In the back of the truck was a large piece of furniture—too big to be a settee and too small to be a full bed. Upholstered in brown corduroy and piled high with fat pillows in flowered slipcovers.

A young woman hopped out of the cab of the truck and sat down at my table, saying, "I was moving today and I brought my couch for you to see. If it could talk, it would tell you quite a few love stories."

During the sixties the girl's mother had come to Seattle to art school. She was in a minimalist phase of her life. Renting a warehouse space to live in, she had bought this couch at an estate sale because she could sit on it during the day and sleep on it during the night. The old woman who had sold it to her said she hated to part with it since she and her husband had courted on it and he had proposed marriage to her on it. The couch already had a part in one family's love story.

The young woman said her mom talked the janitor of the warehouse building into helping her carry the couch into her loft. The young man was working a day job to put himself through law school at night. In time, the two couch-carriers fell in love and ended up sleeping on the couch together.

They married, conceived a child on the couch, and eventually moved into a house, taking the couch with them. A second child was also conceived on the same couch.

In time, the couch was moved to the basement. The children played on it, laid on it recovering from illnesses, did some heavy petting on it as adolescents, and returned to its sanctuary to discreetly recover from beer-bust hangovers during high school.

And now, when the young woman was moving into her own apartment for the first time, her mother had given her the couch—for luck. That was yesterday. The young woman said, "I love this couch. And now I'm looking for the right man to help me move it. Who knows what might happen?" Two young men, who had been listening, immediately volunteered. And off they all went together.

The waitress from the espresso bar had the last word. "Veronica's getting really good with that story—it's the third time she's used it to get that damned couch moved."

—Robert Fulghum

"Women NEED underwear, but women WANT lingerie."

Now there's an opening line with a hook. It's from an article in the June 5 *Forbes* magazine. The president of Victoria's Secret said it. He ought to know—he's got 600 stores and a catalog company with two billion dollars in sales to back it up. I can somewhat attest to this truth myself.

While walking through a mall in Cleveland with some time to kill before a book-signing event, I passed a Victoria's Secret store. Went inside. Looked around. Saleswoman offered to help me. During our conversation she said the store started out as a place where a man could buy lingerie to please a lady. Now, Victoria's Secret appeals to women who want to please themselves—to feel pretty and sexy.

While we were talking I noticed a conservatively dressed older woman who was slowly walking through the store with deliberate dignity. She appraised the racks of sleek garments. And felt the fabrics from time to time. Declining any assistance from the saleswoman, the lady left the store. As I went out the door, she was there staring in at the display in the window.

An hour later, when I walked by again, the woman was still standing there. Dabbing her eyes with a handkerchief. Weeping.

"Excuse me, I couldn't help noticing your distress. Are you all right?"

"No, dammit, I'm not all right. I'm in love." And she poured her story as people will do only with a stranger.

She was seventy-two—a widow. Grown children. Grandchildren. And so forth.

On a whim she had gone to her fiftieth college reunion in St. Louis. And HE was there. The man she had been in love with in college. Deeply in love. Her family had forbidden marriage because the young man was fraternity trash by their standards. She was sent a long way off east to graduate school. She not only lost track of him, she heard he had been killed in the war.

But, here he was. He had prospered in the life insurance business, married, raised a family, and was now widowed himself. And handsome, still. Furthermore, he had come to the reunion to search for her. "WHAM." (I quote the lady.) The years fell away.

They talked, laughed, danced, drank too much punch, and ended up in each other's arms, kissing. "KISSING." (I quote again.) The kissing part made her nervous. The lady said she had urges and feelings she hadn't had in a long time.

When he made some moves in the direction of more than kissing, she declined. Part of her said she was just too old for that sort of thing. But another part of her said it really was her underwear that was too old for that sort of thing.

She went home. They corresponded. They talked by phone. They decided that life was too short to waste and they should get together for a weekend. She invited him to Oberlin, where she lived. He was coming Friday. So here she was at an upscale mall in downtown Cleveland. Weeping outside Victoria's Secret. Feeling neither pretty nor sexy but old and foolish.

I can't tell you the exact outcome of this episode—certainly not what happened on the weekend in Oberlin. It's none of my business. But I can tell you that the gentleman from St. Louis may sooner or later be in for a hell of a surprise.

She won't tell him that some stranger found her weeping in the mall in front of Victoria's Secret and took her by the arm and escorted her inside. Or that the stranger told the saleswoman his aunt needed some nice underthings for a friend about her size who was in love but too embarrassed to come in. No, the black boudoir set should speak for itself.

When women need underwear, but want lingerie, age should never be a problem. The lady may not be as lively as she once was, but she felt as lovely, at least once more, as she ever was. Why should we want to live so long unless such things are possible?

—*Robert Fulghum*

PERSPECTIVE

How would you describe or summarize what you've read?

The title of a book ought to do that in a few words, but finding just the right title for this book was a head-scratching adventure all its own. While True Love *is plain and simple, some of us in the project thought the title could use just a touch of hot sauce or foo-bazz. You might be interested in the titles we did not use. Like the stories in the book, they were too good not to pass on:*

Used Love
Love from the Lost and Found
True Love and False I.D.
Love's a Bitch and It Has Puppies

These titles have merit—all suggest some part of the bittersweet truth about love—but the tent they spread is too small to cover a large crowd of lovers. A cynic might even question the validity of the final choice of True Love—since who really knows or tells the whole truth about love? Well, yes, there's that. Consensus about love is hard to get.

Far be it from me to write a final slam-dunk conclusion to this collection of love stories. Only a fool would write along the lines of All I Really Need to Know about Love I Learned after Kindergarten.

Nobody knows or will ever know everything they need to know about love. Its elusiveness is part of what makes love seductive. Anyone who says they fully understand love is either lying, stupid, or dead.

One can only obey the great law of the heart that says, "As long as you live, love one another and take the consequences."

To Be Continued

We're already well on our way to a sequel to this book.

Telling love stories has become a can-you-top-this contest.

When I asked people to read this manuscript and give me critical feedback, their first response was to say something like, "Let me tell you my love story—I've got one that should have been in this book." As often as not, they did.

If you feel the same way, send me your story.

Keep in mind it must be short, true, and different.

If we can use your story, we'll ask your permission to publish it.

All net royalties from the sale of the book will go to Habitat for Humanity.

Send to:

True Love—Book Two
Suite 155
319 Nickerson Street
Seattle, WA 98109

Be sure to include your name, address and telephone number.

Thanks,
Robert Fulghum

Habitat for Humanity is a worldwide effort to build decent houses for—and with—people who couldn't otherwise afford them. Since its founding twenty years ago by Millard Fuller, its work has taken hold in 1,200 communities in the United States and 48 other countries. Former President Jimmy Carter has helped make Habitat for Humanity one of the most successful self-help endeavors in the world.

If you would like to know more about Habitat for Humanity or would like to participate in its projects and help build a house for someone, write or call:

Habitat for Humanity, International
121 Habitat Street
Americus, GA 31709
1-800-422-4828